THE BERGSONIAN HERITAGE

The Bergsonian Heritage

EDITED WITH AN INTRODUCTION BY

Thomas Hanna

COLUMBIA UNIVERSITY PRESS

NEW YORK AND LONDON 1962

Preface

The essays which form Part One of this book are a product of the Bergson Centennial, which took place October 16, 1959, on the campus of Hollins College. In addition to the desire to commemorate the life and works of one of this century's notable philosophers, it was the special concern of the Centennial to take a long retrospective glance at Henri Bergson, taking stock of the more enduring contributions made by him to present patterns of thought. Bergson was anything but a closet philosopher, and his philosophizing was destined to affect a broad range of human thought. The essays of this book reflect the extensive influence of Bergson not only in philosophy but as well in the rambling bailiwicks of theology and literature.

M. Edouard Morot-Sir, whose essay appraises the philosophical legacy of Bergson, is Cultural Counselor of the French Embassy in the United States and is the Embassy representative in the United States of the French universities. An *agrégé* in philosophy, M. Morot-Sir was, during the forties, professor in the Faculty of Letters at the universities of Lille and Bordeaux, and for two years was professor at the University of Cairo, before returning to Lille. In addition to a host of articles of cosmopolitan range in philosophy, he has published two full-length works in France, *Philosophy and Mysticism* and *Negative Thought: A Logical Study of Its Structure and Processes.* He holds honorary degrees from Middlebury College and Lafayette College.

The consideration of Bergson from the point of view of his effects on theology is made by Jaroslav Pelikan, one of the outstanding younger historians of theology in the United States. Dr. Pelikan was, at the time, professor of Historical Theology in the Federated Theological Faculty of the University of Chicago, and is presently Titus Street Professor of Ecclesiastical History, at Yale University. He is the author of several works in theology, is an editor of the series *Luther's Works,* and in 1959 published *Luther the Expositor.* Also in 1959 Dr. Pelikan received the $12,000 Abingdon Award for his *The Riddle of Roman Catholicism.*

Enid Starkie's contribution to the criticism and biography of French literature is enormous. Dr. Starkie, a member of the Irish Academy of Letters and a Fellow of the Royal Society of Literature, is presently Reader in French Literature at Oxford University. Her sixteen publications include studies of Rimbaud, Gide, and Verhaeren, and her great work on Baudelaire is accepted as a definitive study. During the time of the Centennial, Dr. Starkie was visiting professor of Modern Languages at Hollins College; her presence at the College was a colorful explosion of Irish wit and enthusiasm.

The seven papers in the latter portion of the book are a product of the Bergson Centennial which took place in Paris, May 19, 1959, and was sponsored by the French Philosophical Society and the French Language Society. The theme of these homages was "Bergson et Nous," and the speakers evoked Bergson's past influence on several centers of French intellectual life and his continuing influence into the present time.

Jean Hyppolite, formerly professor of philosophy at the Sorbonne and now director of the École Normale Supérieure, spoke at the École, recalling little known facts of Bergson's life there as a student.

At the Collège de France, its director Marcel Bataillon spoke at the unveiling of a bas-relief plaque of Bergson in Salle 8, the classroom made famous by Bergson. Mr. Bataillon reviews in his paper the influence of Bergson on the Collège and the remarkable enthusiasm with which his lectures were received during Bergson's occupancy of the chairs of Ancient Philosophy and, later, of Modern Philosophy.

The four remaining papers were presented by four of France's most eminent philosophers, in the Grand Amphithéâtre of the Sorbonne. Gaston Berger, a member of the Institut de France, was at the time president of the French Philosophical Society. Gabriel Marcel, also a member of the Institut, was vice-president of the Association des Amis de Bergson. Maurice Merleau-Ponty, of the Collège de France, occupied the chair of Modern Philosophy formerly held by Bergson. Jean Wahl is professor at the Sorbonne, and Vladimir Jankélévitch, also professor at the Sorbonne, was a friend and student of Bergson.

These papers, presented during the American and French Bergson Centennial celebrations, are accompanied by my own remarks about Bergson, which serve not only as an introduction to Bergson and his works but also as a more general appraisal of the Bergsonian heritage.

I feel exceedingly grateful to Suzanne Delorme, general secretary of the Société Française de Philosophie, for her unfailingly patient and friendly aid in expediting the French portion of the book.

My gratitude must be expressed, also, to John R. Everett, at the time president of Hollins College and now chancellor of the Colleges of the City of New York, for the interest and support which made the Centennial possible. And I must express my appreciation to Dean John P. Wheeler, Jr., who thoughtfully and helpfully laid the groundwork for the Bergson program at Hollins College.

THOMAS HANNA

Hollins College
1960

Contents

by Thomas Hanna

THE BERGSONIAN HERITAGE

From his earliest writings to the present time, Henri Bergson has shown himself to be one of the most tantalizing of modern philosophers. "Tantalizing" is just the word for Bergson: for over seventy years his philosophizings have been enormously attractive to a motley variety of persons; however, as soon as one reaches out to grasp his body of thought it seems to disappear within a teasing ambiguity. In the world of academic philosophy there is the simple and honest conviction that a great philosopher influences the thought of his contemporaries and of succeeding generations to the degree that he makes it clear exactly what he is saying and exactly where he stands. Bergson is tantalizing, inasmuch as the continuing influence of his thought goes hand in hand with the fact that he is never systematically and finally clear in what he says, nor is it always possible to pin down where he stands.

There may be a sly wisdom in this. The continuing attractiveness of Bergson's works seems to be very much bound up with a charming ambiguity. If Bergson were less ambiguous and more severely systematic, I fear that his philosophy might already have been dressed and laid out within the quiet mausoleum of philosophical history. But Bergson was not less ambiguous, and he has continued to appeal to a surprisingly varied number of minds. His ambiguity is in this: that he shows all the marks of a mystic, drawing away from the natural world into the surging flux of a non-natural and, perhaps, anti-natural reality; but his other face is that of the avid, open-eyed student of the sciences, insatiably curious about the biological and physical structures of the natural world. Either of these Janus faces is profoundly typical of Bergson. Those who have no doctrinal or emotional patience with the mystic visage may find themselves utterly taken with Bergson's omnivorous absorption of the materials of both experimental and theoretical science. And those who are sick to death of the half-founded pretentiousness of the contemporary scientific world may leap with heels up into the warm rush of his mysticism. Like the Catholic church, Bergson has been capable of receiving all into his bosom.

But no one any longer believes in Janus; our tendency is to deny the existence of such creatures and to settle upon one face to the exclusion of the other. And this is acutely true for twentieth-century philosophy, most particularly in its Anglo-American segment. Janus has been cloven in two, and the visage of subjectivity and mysticism seems to be decisively separated from its rational-empirical counterpart. But whether he has been destroyed is still a matter of speculation, and, accordingly, we should keep in mind that

under these laws, his nature spelled out and exhausted by
these laws. The powerful Marxist delineation of the external determinants of human thought and conduct was
completed by psychoanalysis and psychological determinism, which saw the human creature as a complex organism operated, like all other organisms, by invariable
natural processes. The wave of Darwinism was merely
the confirmation of what was already evident: that the human individual differed from other natural objects or organisms only by degrees of complexity, and thus any notion
of human difference in terms of quality, or freedom, or
nobility was a fiction, now exposed. The moment that this
novel conception of man became operative was like the
moment when a small skiff pushes away from the shores of
a continent: the cultural insights and moral wisdom of the
entire past were denied and abandoned, and the bearers of
a "final" understanding of man launched out loudly and
bravely into a weird and tortured era, hardly conscious of
the enormity of what they had lost. Bergson was a child of
these beginnings, and the task he chose was the difficult one
of reconciling a triumphant but blind understanding of human reality with the past's imperfect but irreplaceable understanding of human reality. That Bergson was not entirely successful in this task is of small importance—no
philosopher worth his salt should ever allow himself to
dream of more than a noble failure—but what is important, as I have said, is that his philosophy is one of the first
great efforts to effect a reconciliation which has not yet
been effected, and which remains the most anxiously and

hotly debated of questions in the mid-twentieth century. Although partially unsuccessful, Bergson's works still remain a treasure house of insights and analyses of this question, and an appraisal of his contribution to present thinking must rest on the great value still to be found in these works, as well as on the more recent philosophical movements which are continuing his task. We should look first at the central insights developed by Bergson during his long writing career, and then compare these with the insights of two highly interesting philosophical movements which, I think, are the special inheritors of Bergson's task: Process Philosophy and Existentialism.

Like that of many another philosopher, Bergson's philosophical career unfolded itself according to the time-honored plan of theme and variations. From the outset he was a thinker with one theme, one conceptual insight which he applied with persistence and enormous imagination to one area after another. It found its first variations in epistemology and psychology, then in metaphysics, then in biological history, then, finally, in morality and history. The theme was unchanging, and no matter which of Bergson's works one picks up the same passacaglia sounds at the base of it. Stated as generally as possible this Bergsonian theme affirms that all experience reveals two categorically distinct realms: that of the organic and that of the inorganic. And this general affirmation is rooted in a clear-cut metaphysical dualism which makes an absolute distinction between two realities: the reality of life or spirit and the reality of matter. That a clearly dualistic metaphysics should be at the base of a highly appealing and presumably "scientifically oriented" philosophy is an extraordinary happening, and the ambiguity of Bergson rests on the enormously resourceful manner in which he has held together this dualism within an argument that is ingenious and persuasive. As in most metaphysical dualisms, Bergson makes what can be termed a male-female distinction: one reality is active, the other passive. Life or spirit is an aggressive reality which has bullied and molded the static reality of matter in creating a distinct and novel realm: that of the organic. Thus, the off-spring of this male ingression is organic life, and it is, perhaps, an obscure echo of Bergson's Jewish patriarchalism that the active spirit is alone sanctioned as the parent of organic life. Put in different terms, spirit seeks to express itself by incarnation within matter, but this incarnation is not a synthesis, it is not a union of two equal realities; rather, organic life is a victory over static matter, spirit's triumphant use of matter to express and realize itself.

This basic metaphysical dualism and its *modus vivendi* of organic and inorganic is the theme sounding throughout Bergson's works. As a theme, it is never expressed by Bergson as baldly as we see it here, but as a theme it is always present, implied and suggested with undoubted clarity. With the lines of this basic conception so clearly drawn, one might wonder how anything so obvious could be developed into a persuasive philosophical position. This is a proper puzzle to wonder at, and I would insist that in understanding this puzzle we encounter in full the genius of

Henri Bergson. The genius of Bergson is not to be found in his basic presuppositions; it is to be found in the manner in which he has argued these basic ideas and organized them in an almost audaciously unique manner. As mentioned already, if Bergson's system of thought is finally unsuccessful, this matters little—this unsuccess hinges primarily on his basic presuppositions. But the success of Bergson and the true measure of his genius is found in the way in which he has argued these difficult presuppositions, and the wealth of insights and analyses he has embedded in these arguments.

Authentic Bergsonism is encountered when we see how he has taken this organic-inorganic dualism and argued it within a broad historical-biological context. Within this context the separation of living beings from static matter appears to be not just a presupposition but has historical and biological support which makes it a compelling viewpoint: Bergson mobilizes theoretical and experimental science to his aid. Organic life, viewed in terms of evolutionary history, is an obvious testimony to the way in which the aggressing spirit has relentlessly molded inorganic matter to its designs. There are evolutionary grades of organic life, clearly indicating the stages of achievement in the creative evolution of life within matter. The stage of torpor is that achieved within plant life; the more advanced stage of instinct is that found in the forms of life crowned by the hymenoptera; and an equally advanced stage is that of intelligence, developed through the vertebrates and perfected with man. Beneath each of these phases of organic life is the ever-present, ever-active impulse of life which has managed in these three evolutionary grades to bully the intractable stuff of matter into a partially successful, partially incomplete incarnation of itself. The human individual must be understood, first, as rooted in the vital impulse of life, and second, his intelligence must be understood strictly for what it is: a limited instrument for encountering a limited aspect of the whole of reality.

It is, then, necessary to note the basic theme of metaphysical dualism, and the basic historical-biological argument of this theme, before one is able to pin down the special way in which human reality is understood in Bergson's philosophy. All of Bergson's works focus on the nature of human reality in the attempt to vindicate the uniqueness and freedom of this reality, but this attempt always takes place against the backdrop of these two basic arguments.

Bergson's first effort in this vindication appeared in 1889 when his doctoral thesis, *Essai sur les données immédiates de la conscience* was published. Later published in English under the title *Time and Free Will*, this work, which remains one of Bergson's most ingenious, was an initial shot at the prevalent attitudes of mechanism and positivism which he saw all about him in the scientific and philosophical world, and it is, to a large extent, a preface to *Matière et Mémoire* (*Matter and Memory*), his next book-length work which appeared in 1896. Together, these two works provided an ample exposition of Bergson's thinking in the areas of psychology, epistemology, and metaphysics, all three of these areas finding their focus of interpretation in perceptive experience, which Bergson describes as being based constitutionally on an enduring, non-material process, as linked with the material world but not explained by or dependent upon the material world. In *Time and Free Will*, qualitative differences were depicted as intensive "facts" (*données*), distinct from extensive facts. The nature of this intensive realm was then described as a "duration" of one's states of consciousness, a fusing together of these states, which is not only an explanation of the inner nature of experience but also is the sole way of explaining the nature of number, of time, and of movement in space. Finally, Bergson opposed his position of dynamism and freedom to that of mechanism and determinism, dynamism recognizing the existence both of free forces and natural laws, mechanism recognizing the existence only of natural laws.

Time and Free Will, a product of Bergson's thirtieth year, is marked by youthful fervor as much as it is by brilliant argumentation. The fervor is evident in Bergson's overenthusiastic peroration on human freedom and his facile distinction between the inner "true self" and the external "social self." In this work, as later in others, Bergson was barely able to rein in his strong evangelical instinct. From this beginning he gave notice that the uniqueness and freedom of human reality were at stake in the philosophical arena, and he, at the precarious age of thirty, challenged the mechanistic systems of thought which were developing apace in the academic halls and in experimental labs. The

distinctive biological and historical themes which were to
be developed in his famous later works are implicit in this,
Bergson's first major effort. The contention that the inner
movement of duration is the very stuff of reality becomes
not only a key for an understanding of the nature of time
and of memory but, inevitably, becomes the interpretive
basis for understanding the evolving character of mankind
as well as of organic life in general. All of organic life is
linked together in time by an enduring reality which relentlessly preserves the past, as this living past gnaws its
way further into the present.

Within a space of seven years, *Matter and Memory* followed Bergson's precocious doctoral thesis somewhat as a
sequel. Whereas the earlier work lists the many specific
experiences made up of intensive, qualitative factors as
well as of extensive, quantitative factors, this sequel ad-
dresses itself to the more general problem of the nature
of perception with the attendant problems of the nature of
memory and of matter. In many respects *Matter and Memory* is Bergson's most interesting work; it is, certainly, the
most tightly argued of all his works. But, unfortunately,
the philosophical worth of the book is somewhat vitiated
by the presence of a large number of turn-of-the-century
findings in clinical and experimental psychology which
now have been either improved upon and superseded or,
in some cases, contradicted. The widespread influence of
Bergson's works was stimulated in large measure by his
constant use of the latest data of the experimental sciences,
but the inherent risk of such philosophizing is that to the

confrontation with matter, it is consciousness projected out into the world of matter. The meaning of the temporal term "present" is quite simply this: the presence of matter before consciousness in the act of perception. The temporal "present" is identified with the perceptual "presentation" of matter to consciousness. Bergson views perception as an active function; it is not a passive observation. By its very nature it is a searching, selective outreach of organisms, appraising the field of matter in terms of action. This pragmatic description of perception fits in with the larger picture of living organisms whose sole function is to develop bodily functions which can adapt to and contend with the material world. Like other bodily functions, perception is designed for action, and, specifically, it is the outreach of the body which scans and assesses the field of action.

But is not memory also a perception? a weak perception which was once strong but has now faded and is stored in the brain? Bergson reasons that if memory is nothing more than a "weak perception," then why is it that we do not confuse a weak sound, for example, with a memory? or why do our memories not seem to be weak perceptions of sounds or colors? The answer, he says, is obvious: memory has nothing to do with the bodily apparatus of perception, it is not in any way a confrontation with what is "present" in the world; it has to do neither with the presence of matter nor with the functions of the body. Memory is obviously an aid to perception, but its source is categorically different: it is part of the enduring reality which is separate from the reality of matter. So then, not only does memory thinking—although he has received little credit for this, the attention being primarily focussed on later Existential thinkers who have continued to make use of this theory.

But, of course, perception is not "pure," nor is memory "pure." *Matter and Memory* analyzes them in terms of their pure and indigenous functions in order to make clear the real linkage of the former with matter and the real separation of the latter from the material and bodily realms. There is no perception without memory and there is no memory except in support of perception. The memory of the past crowds up into present perception, guiding it in appraising possible courses of action. Indeed, memory so crowds and dominates perception that Bergson suggests that we never perceive the present, but only the past. These two functions, separate as to source but unified in their active adaptation of bodily needs to material conditions, are the central elements in Bergson's epistemology. If the function of memory is described as independent of the structure of the brain, this is in no wise a sign of Bergson's naïveté or his contempt for neurology; he is quite aware that memory cannot function without a nervous system, that without a living body there would be no memory. But, as he puts it, if a hat is hanging on a peg, this does not mean that the peg accounts for the hat, or causes the hat to be, or can be used to describe the hat. As Bergson sees it, the functions of memory are enormously broader than the functions of the nervous system: the latter does no more than trace the bare outlines of the former. The skeletal tracings of the nervous system are indisputably related to the functions of memory, but these tracings are not and should never be asserted as identical with and exhaustive of memory's functions. The middle sections of *Matter and Memory* involve some clever discussions of the contradictions which arise when one tries to treat memory as a purely physiological fact. With examples of various types of oral and auditory aphasia, Bergson notes the impossibility of claiming that memories are located in any specific cell group in the brain; one cannot say "where" memories are. Some types of aphasia may suggest that if there are lesions of the brain, memories are automatically destroyed, but Bergson takes pains to show that it is not the memories themselves which are destroyed but, rather, the ability to use, recognize, or communicate these memories for practical bodily activities. If an aphasiac, for example, can hear and understand all words except those beginning with an f, and if his hearing itself is not impaired, then this does not mean he has forgotten the letter f, but, quite the contrary, that it is automatically recognized and selected as a sound which is not to be responded to. This is an excellent example of what Jean-Paul Sartre was later to call "bad faith," and it is worthwhile noting that Sartre was not the originator of the reasoning behind this famous term.

If *Les Données immédiates* and *Matière et Mémoire* were the enunciators of Bergson's basic theme, the first great variation on this theme was the extraordinary *L'Evolution Créatrice*, which, in one of his letters to Bergson, evoked from William James the judgment that the book was a "marvel," "a real wonder in the history of philosophy. . . . There is so much that is absolutely new that it will take a long time for your contemporaries to assimilate it." *Creative Evolution,* with its vitalistic interpretation of biological evolution and its catch phrases and analogies, appeared like a rocket in 1907 and soared cleanly over the walls of the academy into the ken of a general public. This, the third of Bergson's major works, quickly became one of the rarities of philosophical literature, a smash. If not actually read by everyone, it was, like the Bible, known by everyone and quoted by all. Before its appearance, the only published work to come from Bergson following *Matter and Memory* was the little essay on laughter, entitled *Le Rire.* This essay with its ingenious interpretation of laughter and the comic and with its brief, *en passant* disclosure of Bergson's theory of esthetics, was the first instance of Bergson's adaptation of his basic theme to the areas of biology and anthropology. It is also an instance of Bergson's troubling ambiguity. Bergson sees the essentials of the comic in whatever smacks of automism and mechanical inelasticity in human life. The comic is inherent in what is habitual and blindly unadaptable to new conditions; as such, human unadaptability is a minor threat to society, and laughter is the involuntary social response which restrains and corrects such eccentricities.

This is an interesting and even persuasive theory of the comic. As to its truth, there is simply no way of telling; this is the kind of theory which can never be more than "interesting"—it is in no way subject to validation. Even so, this would not count against Bergson's theory of the comic if his theory were consistent with the entirety of his philosophy. Unfortunately, it is not. Considerably later, in his *Two Sources of Morality and Religion*, Bergson contends that the primitive social instinct is that of conformity and habit—a parallel in human society to the inelastic hive tendency instinctive in the highly developed hymenoptera. Thus, in this later work, social morality is seen to be a protective reaction which pressures each individual in society into habitual, unvarying actions. So then, in *Laughter* society is described as constitutionally fearful of automatism, and in *The Two Sources* society is described as constitutionally fearful of any threat to automatism within the group. This inconsistency is further deepened when Bergson contends that laughter is intellectual in nature and devoid of emotional content; but in *The Two Sources* intelligence, as such, is seen to be a threat to the social group—not a protection as suggested by *Laughter*—and it is to defend itself against the innovations of intelligence, says Bergson, that primitive societies instinctively create myths which confound the straight-line movement of intelligence which otherwise would destroy the closed circle of society. On the face of it, this is a simple contradiction; Bergson never resolved it, nor, indeed, did he ever seem aware of it. In a somewhat complex and arbitrary manner, Bergson may have felt there was not at all a contradiction here: there are varying nuances given by Bergson to the meaning of instinct, residual instinct, intelligence, social self, inner self, and "life," so that in a complex juggling of these meanings he may have found a way of justifying this apparent contradiction. Whether or not he could have unknotted this problem matters little; what does matter, unfortunately, is that these large areas of inconsistency hover above the whole of Bergson's philosophy like a pall.

For all its acclaim and despite its obvious intention to transform the general lines of biological theory, *Creative Evolution* succeeded in creating perhaps one generation of vitalists in biology, a generation which now has all but vanished. Viewed from a distance of half a century what was important about *Creative Evolution* was the way in which great and hopeful prospects were suddenly opened up for a meaningful, nontheological conception of history and for a wholesome respect between the proponents of scientific intelligence and those of intuitive understanding. For a long moment, the universe seemed large enough for both science and poetry and not only that, but in *need* of them both. This is to say that although *Creative Evolution* was a brilliant failure in biological theory, it succeeded in another way by loosening up the scientific and philosophical thinking of the 1900s and offering serious thinkers a broad perspective in which humanitarian concerns were not swallowed up by dispassionate objectivity. If Bergson's own viewpoint seems no longer tenable, still the humanitarian implications of *Creative Evolution* have survived and, in ways impossible to calculate, have directly and indirectly spawned new philosophical viewpoints which continue to evaluate the modern world with the same broad perspective that was characteristic of Bergson.

Only two major works followed *Creative Evolution.* One

habit are not a product of society as such; rather, they are products of individuals within that society who, abandoning the instinctive imperative of social conformity, aspire to a universality which bursts out of the tight circle of group habit and group self-preservation. The source of this aspiration is not in social "instinct"; it is in "feeling," a feeling of the vital impulse of life itself which is universal, expansive, and liberating. As Bergson describes it, social morality evolves in ever expanding circles. From time to time, a prophetic leader leads his society in the direction of his own expansive aspiration: the old circle of habits is broken and expanded into a more universal social morality, and the "opened" society ossifies once more with its broadened but again static morality. The next expansion waits upon the next prophet. Thus, social changes are not due to a revolt against the past, but rather to an evolution from it, a continuous line of expansion from the narrow toward the universal. Like Jesus of Nazareth, prophets do not come to destroy the law but to fulfill it.

In this way Bergson applies his concerns to social history, and in *The Two Sources* he links this theory to his biological theories with the notion that species evolution has reached its ultimate in the static society, and that evolution, henceforth, can take place only by means of individuals. The vital impulse of life, which has driven and bullied matter to its final possibilities of organic life, will continue its mission through the moral prophet and the religious mystic. These mystic heroes gain their expansive visions not through intelligence but through absorption in the di-

If, for example, the notion of a creative evolution of organic life is now passé, the notion of a creative process of nature is not at all passé, and Alfred North Whitehead, who is the most influential spokesman for Process Philosophy, has provided a philosophical system of considerable attractiveness to both the world of philosophy and that of science. In truth, Whitehead's thought is weighted heavily with Bergson's own concerns and is studded with insights and arguments directly traceable to Bergson. Speaking broadly, Whiteheadeanism is an expansion of the relatively simple conception of creative evolution, an expansion which goes beyond biology into the realms of physics and mathematics. Bergson's limitation was that he restricted the notions of duration and evolution to organic life—an idea increasingly intolerable to physical scientists in the twentieth century. Whitehead, in a more complex way, has included all of inorganic nature within his conception of process and by this has rehabilitated the Bergsonian ideas of duration, memory, creative process, and teleology. Whitehead has made persuasive use of these ideas for the simple reason that as a metaphysician, he succeeded where Bergson fell short. With his expansive philosophical outlook, Bergson, from the beginning, strained toward a systematic metaphysical position, but this he never achieved. Bergson succeeded in arriving at scientific hypotheses instead of metaphysical statements. As mentioned already, this was Bergson's attractiveness as well as his ultimate limitation as a philosopher. In his epistemology, in his evolutionary doctrines, and in his social-historical doc-

trines Bergson persistently took hypothetical positions
which were intended to transform scientific experimentation and which, by nature, were subject to an ultimate verification or rejection by the sciences. Bergson's fate as a
philosopher has largely been determined by scientists, not
by other philosophers. His strong interest in Einstein lay
in his having found a kindred spirit who was making the
same theoretical innovations in the inorganic sciences as
Bergson was in the organic sciences. Unfortunately, Einstein's theories gradually received increasingly dramatic
verification, while Bergson's theories wilted on the vine.
The best explanation for Bergson's impressive failure as
a scientific theoretician is the same as that for his failure
to succeed as a metaphysician: he was not sufficiently con-
versant with the outlook and problems of mathematics and
physics. The field of metaphysics always has and likely always will be the playground of mathematicians and physicists. This is manifestly the case with Whitehead: he has
achieved a more systematic metaphysical framework for
Bergson's concerns chiefly because his training and outlook
inevitably pointed him toward the elemental nature and
structure of reality.

It is a remarkable event in philosophical history that
Henri Bergson constructed such impressive conceptual
schemes, inasmuch as he not only was focussed away from
the mathematical-physical sciences, but, in truth, was concerned with the organic and social sciences primarily as a
means of arguing his convictions about human existence.
The focal point of Bergson's philosophy is the nature of

man, the consciousness of man, and the freedom of man. In this respect, the authentic inheritors of the Bergsonian tradition are not the Process Philosophers but the Existential thinkers.

A perplexing question for many persons is whether Bergson is an Existentialist or is perhaps some kind of proto-Existentialist. For a host of reasons, I believe that it would make little sense to identify him with the Existential movement, certainly the prime reason being Bergson's characteristic desire to validate his ideas through empirical and rational means. The concerns are basically the same—human existence, consciousness, and freedom—but Bergson always makes the effort to treat these areas within a naturalistic framework, nature understood in the Bergsonian sense as being the conjunction of the real stuff of matter with the equally real stuff of duration. The attitude of Existential philosophers is much more that of a strict attention to the nature of individual existence described in its own terms and in its own categorical differences from that which is extra-individual, without being concerned to justify this description in either empirical or rational terms. Even as Whiteheadeanism gives Bergsonism a final impersonal and universal focus which it did not possess, so does Existentialism give Bergsonism a final personal and individual focus which it did not possess. Bergson's insights survive incorporated within viewpoints other than his own and more sharply drawn than his own.

For example, Bergson's theory of perception, developed in *Matter and Memory*, has become an important element in Existential thought. Existential thinkers have, for the most part, reacted strongly to the main tendencies in Western philosophy and theology. One particular tendency they (and Whitehead) reject is the "mind-body" dichotomy of Cartesian thought, a basic split which is still stuck in the craw of contemporary philosophy and psychology. The Existential position is that sense perception of an object is, in fact, of that object; perception is exactly what it is immediately taken to be: an encounter of a real perceiver with a real object within a unitary reality called perception. The Cartesian tendency, which applies simple-minded surgery to the reality of perception, leaving an unmendable and inexplicable separation between something called "mind" and something called "matter"—this erroneous separation is seen by Existentialists to be the product not of an analysis of perception qua perception but rather to be a logical analysis of the physical processes presumed to be the corollary of the reality of perception. Therefore an observer, following blindly in the Cartesian tradition of psychology, will make the inevitable statement that visual perception is not of the "real" material object "out there" but, rather, is a product of one's retinal sensations and is not to be confused with the independent objective reality that is prior to and distinct from retinal impressions. Thus, is "mind" split off from "matter" as the result of what seems to many persons to be an indisputable fact of analysis. But Existential thought has succeeded in making its point that the reality of any man's sense perception is completely devoid of any data of a "split": when one views any analysis of perception must begin with the reality of perception and not with an analytical corollation of it. Applied to the problem of perception, this is only one instance of the typical Existential viewpoint that reality is never anything but my conscious reality in the world; anything extraneous to my conscious reality may be interesting but it is not "serious," nor is it fully real.

Bergson shared this view of the unified reality of perception, understanding perceptive experience to be a real contact with the reality of matter, and he defends this view extensively in *Matter and Memory*. But this view of perception should not be confused with Bergson's peculiar conception of "intuition," developed later in *Creative Evolution, Introduction to Metaphysics* and still other of his essays. When he speaks of "intuition" Bergson is not speaking of the perceptual unity of the observer and his object but rather of a special act of consciousness which is a way of knowledge and not a sense perception. In intuition one has, by withdrawing into oneself, attained a sympathetic relationship with an object: one has a living "feeling" of the object, not a "representation." Intuition is, then, of a different order than perception; Bergson developed his notion of intuition to the deficit of his earlier understanding of perception. This was a parallel development of his biological philosophy, wherein "intuition" is the human manifestation of that internal sympathy of relationships which, in other organic life, is called "instinct." Unfortunately, Bergson leaves us confused as to the exact nature of intuition; we know that it involves a conscious relaxa-

tion into the inner flow of life, but we become confused in
specifying whether this involves a knowledge of other living beings (the notion of instinct in *Creative Evolution*),
the knowledge of all inorganic as well as organic beings
(the notion of metaphysics in *Introduction to Metaphysics*),
or simply the knowledge of the vital impulse of life which
underlies all things (the notion of mysticism in *The Two
Sources of Morality and Religion*). Whatever the problems with Bergson's conception of intuition, this should
not blind us to the worth of his theory of perception, which
continues to make itself felt in the contemporary philosophical world.

But in carrying on Bergson's special attitude toward human consciousness, Existentialism has not only developed
his theory of perception, but has, interestingly enough, developed his pragmatic theory of perception. Bergson understood perception to be founded in the needs of action
rather than of knowledge; perception is a natural organic
activity that surveys the environing world in terms of possible actions of the organism on that world or possible
threats from it. Hence, perception, motivated by the practical needs for action, is selective in its appraisal of the
world: what one perceives is a function of what one needs;
what is not of practical importance to the organism is edited
out of perception. Taking together Bergson's two theories
of perception, we have the following position: if perception is of the real world (and not just a distorted, sensual
echo) and if human perception is inescapably governed
by the needs of one's nature (which thus orders and selects

the reality of the world), then "reality" can only be defined as that which is "real" to us in the promises and threats of the world. This notion that the nature of the real world is partially contingent upon the specific needs of human existence is a prominent theme in the philosophies of Heidegger, Jaspers, Sartre, Buber, and is implicit in all of Existential thought. Heidegger's *Dasein* discloses a world which is what it is, because it has been disclosed to the *Dasein*. Sartre's *Pour-Soi* discovers the reality of negation in the world, a nothingness which the *Pour-Soi* itself contributes to its relationship with the world.

So, then, Bergson's special concerns for the nature of human consciousness have been continued within later systems of thought. The attitudes toward human nature and human freedom are also present in Existentialism, but they have undergone much more extensive transformation. The uniqueness of human nature was seen by Bergson to be predicated on two points: the distinction of organic nature from inorganic matter, and the privileged position of the human creature in respect to all other stages of evolutionary development. Existentialism, of course, makes a radical reduction of human uniqueness to the uniqueness of each individual existence. In his earlier psychological and epistemological works, Bergson had the possibility of moving toward this kind of individualistic position, but it was drowned in the flood of new ideas developed in *Creative Evolution*.

Bergson's conception of human freedom has been reflected somewhat more directly in Existentialist literature.

If we divest the notion of duration from its evolutionary overtones, we have a conception of the free, inner reality of human consciousness which is largely the same as that of the Existentialists. The main theme of Existential philosophy is that one exists in the world and is part of it, but at the same time one cannot be completely defined in terms of the world or exhausted by it. Existentialism sees the individual as a spectator to his own inescapable involvement in the natural processes of the world, and in this fact of "spectatorship," there is revealed the unique detachment and freedom characteristic of one's consciousness of oneself and one's world. Bergson's theory of the real self as an inner duration (rather than a spatialized object) is, taken in its bare sense, a basic theme of Existential philosophy, and is especially amenable to the attitudes of theological Existentialists who see this duration embedded in an eternal life principle.

As a summary statement about the Bergsonian heritage, it would be fair to say, then, that Bergson's early works (*Time and Free Will* and *Matter and Memory*) have special psychological and epistemological themes which Existentialism continues to develop, and that Bergson's later, more expansive works have metaphysical implications that have been most successfully realized in the Process Philosophy of Alfred North Whitehead and his followers.

The interest in "Bergsonism," already curtailed to a minimum, is destined to fade away entirely. And even though his insights and arguments will continue to effect their presence in philosophy, Bergson's characteristic biological and historical systems will come to be only engagingly interesting failures. Bergson's philosophy had a rocket-like beginning, and it blazed up, opening new and more expansive vistas than we could have hoped for; if we have seen the rocket exhaust itself and follow downward on a sad and ageless trajectory, it should not be too much of a disappointment. The contribution of Bergson is that he made a whole generation look up and see the possibility of a world large enough and tolerant enough to include the goods of varied viewpoints, varied endeavors, and varied types of men. A man's aspirations must always be counted more important than his achievements, otherwise no man is worth more than his tomb. If the traditions of philosophy remain largely unaffected by "Bergsonism," they do not, I believe, remain impervious to Henri Bergson himself, for the man Bergson brought to philosophy an eloquence, an imagination, an expansiveness, and a concern for the value and uniqueness of men that is as rare as it is irreplaceable. If this much of the Bergsonian heritage is not worth carrying on, then, surely, philosophy itself is not worth carrying on.

PART ONE

The Bergson Centennial
at Hollins College

by Edouard Morot-Sir

WHAT BERGSON MEANS TO US TODAY

In 1912 John Dewey wrote: "No philosophic problem will ever exhibit just the same face and aspect that it presented before Professor Bergson invited us to look at it in its connections with duration as a real and fundamental fact." In 1913 Edouard Le Roy, the most devoted of Bergson's disciples, exclaimed enthusiastically: "Beyond any doubt, and by common consent, Mr. Henri Bergson's work will appear to future eyes among the most characteristic, fertile and glorious of our era. It marks a never-to-be-forgotten date in history." A little further, Le Roy asserts that this philosophical revolution is equal in importance to that effected by Kant, or even, by Socrates.

It was over half a century ago that these appreciations, and many other similar ones coming from the greatest minds of that period, greeted the publication of the philosopher's works. Can we today ratify these opinions? Or, at least, how should we formulate them, in the name of a not-so-distant posterity?

Let us turn to the professional philosophers for an opin-

ion. They are unanimous in recognizing in Bergson one of
the greatest philosophers of our century. Such was the opinion expressed in May, 1959, by the French Philosophical
Society in a ceremony at the Sorbonne commemorating the
hundredth anniversary of the birth of the author of *Creative Evolution*. Such a tribute, however, is too general. It
is true that philosophy students read the works of Bergson
and that professors explain the different aspects of his doctrine. What is then the significance of this recognition? We
may interpret it this way: Bergson belongs to our past; he
has become for us a classic of the history of philosophy;
one must be acquainted with his thought, as one must ac-
quaint oneself with Kant or Rousseau. On reading the
speeches in praise of Bergson given in Paris a few months
ago, I was struck by the fact that their judgment is almost
identical: The influence exerted by Bergson in his lifetime
has been decisive and profound. As it has been said, his effect is felt "in all avenues of thought today." Moreover, his
own authentic personal greatness is recognized, and thus
he assumes an exemplary value. For generations to come,
he will be an ideal model for philosophers; he has given
the example of a life entirely and truly devoted to metaphysical research.

Such eulogies, however, can imply severe criticism.
Bergson is thus relegated to the past, irrevocably separated
from present-day life. Some have gone so far as to say that
he belongs to the nineteenth century. In short, should we
consider that Bergson's thought deserves to be embalmed,
or on the contrary should we consider him as one of us,

as a direct ancestor who still has something to say to us
and can be our guide?

Such is, in my opinion, the real problem we have to deal
with today, a problem concerning the present and the future, not a problem of determining what rank Bergson
should have in the Pantheon of philosophers. This is why
I should like you to forget the very ambiguous notion of
influence and substitute that of presence. You may well
think that this is a mere substitution of words, the real
problem remaining the same. I am convinced however that
the change of words indicates a change of attitude towards
the same problem of the survival of a philosopher's thought.
But how can we measure at a given moment of human
history the presence, and we might say, the weight of presence of a human being and of his work? It seems to me that
simultaneously we can use two means, two measures, one
objective, and the other subjective. We often pass from one
to the other without realizing it. The first one is that of the
historian who proceeds like a detective, picking up clues,
finding here and there a person's actual presence, and thus
determining a certain historical dimension peculiar to an
individual. The second one is that of the philosopher, in-
different to the historical background of a work, but seeking in it whatever assistance it may provide for our present-
day thinking and whatever solution it may offer to our
present-day problems. Thus, in this perspective, one may
speak of the enduring character of the work which has escaped the dialogue of the dead imposed by the historian in
order to enter another dialogue, a dialogue with the living.

I apologize for this long preamble on a question of methodology. I thought it was necessary if we wish to avoid a study of influences, always of doubtful value. I shall now take the point of view of the historian and then the point of view of the philosopher as they have just been defined.

An historian may verify objectively the following facts. First of all, today there is no visible Bergsonian movement, or Bergsonian school, as there have been for example a Cartesian movement in the second part of the seventeenth century, a post-Kantian and an Hegelian movement in the nineteenth century. Then everybody will agree that the philosophical thought of the last fifteen years can be divided into three main trends: Logical Positivism, which through its many manifestations tries to give to science, as the only source of truth, a logical and legal status; Marxism, with its orthodoxy and revisionists; finally, Existentialism. Who would be so bold as to detect some Bergsonian element in the various expressions of the three tendencies now dominating the scene? The answer may be less definite in the case of Existentialism, which has had and still has important representatives in France; and it would be tempting to suppose that philosophers such as Sartre and Gabriel Marcel and even Heidegger are descendants of Bergson, who opened the way for them. However, a first look at the main Existentialist themes reveals an opposition to Bergsonism. We might even believe that Sartre, for example, has dreamed of being an anti-Bergson.

As a reaction against a psychology of empiricist origin,

against an atomistic psychology claiming to be scientific, and also against the beginnings of psycho-physics, Bergson emphasized the dynamism of mental life, its originality as temporal reality, as duration opposed to space, its autonomy as creative power and freedom, its profound unity and its continuity which does not allow any gaps and cannot be reduced to atoms such as sensations and images. Hence the meaning of the famous and now banal comparisons which Bergson used from the start in his *Time and Free Will*— mental life is an inner life flowing like a stream, it is a stream of consciousness, it is a flame, it is a deep pool covered with dead leaves, it is a spring which is under tension and then released. With the phenomenology of Husserl, on the contrary, appears the idea of a consciousness whose unity consists in its relation-to-something. Hence, the now famous remark, inherited from absolute idealism: consciousness is always the consciousness of something. In short, for Husserl and his followers, consciousness is at once the consciousness of the world of objects and of other human beings. It means nothing except in its relation to this world and to others. With Sartre, this philosophy of consciousness, first dramatized by Heidegger, becomes a theory of man as a human being cast into the world, absorbed by the world, who can assert his freedom only in the revolt of a negation. Sartre wishes to introduce after Heidegger and against the entire classical philosophy of which Bergson would be the last representative, a new ontology which would be in fact a "meontology," that is to say, a theory of existence founded on the idea of nothing-

ness and no longer on that of Being. It may be recalled that
Bergson, in his *Creative Evolution,* had tried to prove that
the idea of non-Being was second and the product of an
artificial dialectic of the intelligence as a fabricator of antinomies. Moreover, with his well-known distinction of the
"in-itself" and the "for-itself," Sartre considers consciousness as an empty power, tension towards negation, which is
revealed in a series of breaks, but which hardens and
freezes in its inevitable and inescapable relation with the
world of objects and the others.

There is no need to continue this analysis further: the
two attitudes seem to be diametrically opposed. Basically,
this is a conflict of philosophical methods. With Bergson,
there is an attempt to go beyond intellectual analysis and
to recapture by an act of intuitive sympathy the being and
the existence in their original quality. With Sartre, it is the
most subtle attempt of intelligence to describe the infinitely
complex interplay of continuous relationships which occur
at every moment between men and the world and which
constitute the real life of the mind.

But this is not only a matter of opposition between two
philosophical temperaments. Is it not also a conflict of
generations and of metaphysical sensibility? Our epoch
appears to be anti-Bergsonian. It is full of violent and dramatic contrasts, torn by antinomies—political, social, cultural antinomies. Marxism advocates a revolution which
in its wake will bring about the birth of a new type of man.
Everywhere, in all countries, whatever their moral and
religious ideals may be, society exerts its pressure on the

individual, attracting his attention by all the means of pub-
licity at its disposal; and it seems to justify Sartre when he
denounces this kind of constant bleeding of the psyche
which he identifies with the very life of the mind. Inti-
macy, which for Bergson was the very quality of the
psyche, disappears. Moreover, as I said before, Bergson
condemns the antinomies as artificial productions of an intelligence turned towards the external world and seems to
escape into easy optimism when he invites us to rise above
these contradictions to find the serene unity of the spirit.
It is difficult then for a man of our time to accept this idyl-
lic picture. All of us have been insidiously influenced by
Hegel's dialectics. Finally, it could be added that the developments of scientific psychology in the last fifty years
hardly justify Bergson. Is there a psychologist who has
ever followed the advice of the author of *L'Essai* when he
underscored the irreducible opposition between spiritual
quality and the spatial quantity? The famous behaviorist
and Gestalt theories owe nothing to Bergson. Freud's psychoanalysis is undoubtedly much nearer, but it originated
about the same time, and it is well known that in its most
recent developments it has moved away from Bergsonism
and has come closer to phenomenology and Existentialism.

Here is, you will say, a negative balance sheet which is
a condemnation. Is Bergson's presence today only felt in
contrasts? I do not think so, and now I shall try to prove
that the preceding oppositions may be more superficial
than is claimed by many present-day philosophers.

In my opinion, Bergson is still among us. First, he is so

indirectly by certain themes which have become so familiar to us that we have forgotten their Bergsonian origin. Second, he is so in a direct way, in our conception of certain philosophical problems that we cannot avoid posing in terms defined by Bergson at the beginning of this century.

Since Descartes, the problem of mind as consciousness has been at the heart of all European philosophies. Existentialism is but the last metamorphosis to date of the extraordinary history of the Western culture in search of its spiritual vocation and its mission in defining human mind. Now, today, it has become impossible to approach this problem without adopting certain attitudes which we have inherited from Bergson and which appear as a filigree in our philosophical thinking.

It is true that Existentialism came into being when Kierkegaard revolted against the Hegelian system, thus causing the framework of traditional psychology to burst and giving the romantic revolution its modern aspect. However, the rebirth of Kierkegaard after 1930 in Europe was possible only because already Bergsonism had borne its first fruits. Bergson's role was to purify. He prepared minds for existential dialectics. It may be banal to say that he restored the sense of quality in philosophical thought, and also that he called our attention to those aspects of consciousness which escape a purely intellectual analysis. By emphasizing the oppositions between quality and quantity, mathematical time and concrete duration, continuity and discontinuity, the social self and the inner self, Bergson made possible existential descriptions. The opposition

First, there is the problem of the existence of extra-scientific knowledge. Today it is difficult to consider metaphysics in the manner of Aristotle or even Descartes and to make it the foundation of the sciences. There remains the proud attitude of the Positivists, for those, at least, who can be satisfied with Positivism. What about the others? The Bergsonian approach to the problem, it seems to me, is the most alive today. Science is not the extension of metaphysics; it tends to be sufficient unto itself, to give itself its own principles and to establish its truths in relation to a reality, i.e., to a universe which it explores in two directions—the direction of the infinitely small and that of the infinitely great. I do not claim that we should accept the famous theory of a scientific intelligence turned towards space, conceiving more and more subtle geometric systems. But we must, along with Bergson, start from the following fact: there is a science with its truths and its capabilities, and it has an autonomous existence. Moreover, and by virtue of this attitude towards science, the problem of the existence of metaphysics can be formulated in Bergsonian terms. The philosopher of the *Mind-Energy* invites us to seek a knowledge which is parallel to science, as positive as science is, but which is of a different kind and is turned towards another reality, which we shall call the mind, with its own resources of energy. And the well-known doctrine of intuition, so poorly understood in Bergson's lifetime, takes on a clearer meaning in this perspective: it is the awareness of a reality which is not spatial and yet can be explored and described. Following Bergson,

Max Scheler and René Le Senne have recently introduced the notion of Value to give a new life to spiritualism. But the meta-physical intuition of Value which inspires our thoughts and motivates our actions is a consequence of the intuition of the *élan vital* and of the inner self. Heidegger, in developing his metaphysics of Being, also found on his way the same sympathy with an "authentic" existence which does not allow itself to be bound by the necessities of a life governed by science and its techniques. Today there is a whole literature which boasts of denouncing the evils of scientific organization when, as a matter of fact, it does nothing but give common expression, often incompletely and awkwardly, to this anguish and kind of questioning, to which Bergson gave form in a way unknown before his time.

Moreover, Bergson did not limit himself to just stating the problem of original metaphysical experience. For him, it is an experimentation. It is no longer simply a question of language, but of action. The philosopher must, himself, promote the metaphysical life. I do not know if such a task can be truly realized, but I know that the possibility must be entertained. If there is a crisis of philosophy in the world today, it may be because too many philosophers, after becoming aware of this possibility, avoid their responsibilities and accept a method which is a compromise between reflection and description. Bergson showed that there was no metaphysical knowledge without a metaphysical life, just as there can be no science without experimentation. Such is the starting point of the contemporary problem of the coexistence and relationship between science and philosophy. This is a pressing problem, because it conditions our moral and religious life, and it is our most dramatic problem, because it should be at the root of any philosophy of education.

There is yet another present-day problem which has come to us in Bergsonian terms: the problem of life. I am aware of the fact that most biologists refuse to acknowledge Bergson as a master and claim that they owe nothing to the philosopher of *Creative Evolution.* They are undoubtedly right when it comes to their techniques and hypotheses. Their true ancestor remains Claude Bernard. Yet it is well known that Bergson considered himself a disciple of Claude Bernard and that he wrote a penetrating essay on the author of *Introduction to Experimental Medicine.* Bergson gave a metaphysical dimension to the theme of "the vital principle" governing living organisms. Thanks to him, our epoch has become aware of the problem of life as an original, autonomous problem. Here also, as before, he introduced new elements which we cannot fail to take into account. Once more I do not claim that we must all follow Bergson. Yet Bergson taught us that we must go beyond the classical dualism and conflict between mechanism and finalism. Studies like those of Alexis Carrel and Schrodinger seemingly owe nothing to Bergson. I do not believe, however, that they could have been written before *Creative Evolution.*

When he denounced the artificial character of an antithesis which opposed Lamarck and Darwin, as well as their disciples, Bergson reinjected into reflection on life a new freedom and boldness which has benefited even those who seek to define a more subtle biological mechanism or a vital dynamism endowed with organizing power. Also, it is true that there is no common measure between the *élan vital* and the present hypothesis of the transformists: these theories move on different planes of thought. But here again, however, Bergson's role was a purifying one in that it lifted the weight of a crushing past off from philosophical imagination. Finally, for professional philosophy, the fate of *Creative Evolution* took a curious turn. When it first appeared and for some 30 years after, many philosophers looked upon *Creative Evolution* as a metaphysical novel consisting of poetic flights and very vague ideas. I still remember one of my philosophy professors saying to his class in 1930, "This book by M. Bergson cannot be taken seriously. The philosophical method should be more rigorous and less fanciful." Such, indeed, is the way the book strikes us: it is brilliant and glib. However, today we have penetrated under the surface and discovered a rigorous analysis of the fundamental ideas of biological instinct and intelligence, of life and matter in relation to the principle of the degradation of energy (law of entropy) which Bergson then called the most metaphysical principle in nature. In making life the necessary starting point of any philosophical reflection on man, Bergson, at the beginning of this century, gave a solemn warning, too often misinterpreted at present: we must consider the striking paradox of man who has his roots in the animal kingdom and yet creation and consequently a principle of energy, which allows one to place man in nature and at the same time invites him to rise above it.

To help us understand this principle and give it a living value, I do not know of any better guide at present than Bergson. For the man of today, there are three main centers of reflection. The first is on the plane of biological thought insofar as it seeks to go beyond the findings of science after assimilating them. A French philosopher, Raymond Ruyer, has shown Bergson's importance in this respect. Man finds himself an obscure energy which makes his body an unlimited source of potential action, an energy which is constantly struggling against physical inertia. Bergson undoubtedly was the first to have so fully grasped the meaning of our body as an immediate and direct instrument and tool. Such, I believe, is the source to which we have to return in order to avoid easy romantic notions about existence, as well as the notion of human work and its technique. In short, we must rediscover the significance and natural impulse of our body, and Bergson can help us do it.

The second center of reflection, in my opinion, lies on the social plane. Undoubtedly, the political philosophy of the eighteenth century gave us the principles of personal freedom and free exchange; but the increase in human population and, parallel to it, the development of industrial techniques since then, requires a reinterpretation of society as a storehouse of potential energies. Here, once more, we feel the presence of Bergson. I do not need to give as example the sociology suggested in the *Two Sources of Morality and Religion,* but Bergson does offer us there a new element of reflection as a point of departure, that of a social inertia on the one hand which is characterized by a necessary equilibrium, and, on the other, a revolutionary creation which has nothing to do with a deterministic and historical dialectic but which relates rather to the mystery of human creativity and consequently to those whom Bergson chose to call heroes and saints. I do not believe that we should keep the famous distinction between "closed" and "open" societies; but it is not possible to solve the problem of the relationship between the individual and society without thinking over social inertia and the creative spirit. It is not enough to champion the cause of an élite or to defend the rights of an aristocracy of intellectuals and artists. Once more, it is necessary to return to the source of our difficulties and try to understand the exact meaning of social energy.

Finally, the third center of reflection is that of the mind itself. Today there is a tendency to say that the man chiefly responsible for the reorientation of European thought was and still is Sigmund Freud. It is a fact that contemporary psychology has been more markedly influenced by Freud than by Bergson. But Freud has been the explorer of the dark recesses of the human mind. Unquestionably, his work has been a liberating force, and yet, in my opinion, it remains negative. Bergson, on the contrary, opened the way to another kind of exploration—the exploration of the energy of our personal mind. Such could be the point of

departure for a revolutionary psychology and pedagogy.
And such will be, I hope, the task of tomorrow. This is why
I am convinced Bergson's future will be richer than his
past.

I do not wish to elaborate any longer on my personal
convictions. My main objective was to try and prove the
inexhaustible vitality of Bergson's thought. It surrounds
us; it beckons us towards new progress. I have not mentioned the impact of his thought in fields other than philosophy because his influence is always diffuse and hard
to grasp. At any time, a philosopher's influence is communicated in an indirect way through channels which are
difficult to identify. Thus people have pointed out the Bergsonism of Marcel Proust who, in his turn, is the source of
the contemporary novel as a whole. In Europe, the surrealist movement, born after the First World War, seems to
owe a greater debt to Rimbaud and Freud than to Bergson.
But one may ask if the surrealist call to automatic writing
and unique love is not essentially more Bergsonian than
Freudian. I shall leave to others the task of solving these
historical questions which, in order to be resolved, require
a perspective still lacking today. All I know is this: philosophy still needs Bergson today. His genius lies essentially in his metaphysical sensibility and his quiet intellectual daring. Without trying to be paradoxical, we can say
that he is perhaps more alive today than he was yesterday.
Separated from his past and from his own epoch, he is
nearer to us than many living philosophers.

As a conclusion, allow me to remind you that Bergson,

of all European philosophers, is the one who, without doubt, has best sensed the great and permanent values of the United States, and that he is a man whose thinking is closest to the American. He bridges spiritualism and pragmatism and rises above the national barriers which too often give a touch of provincialism to many philosophies of the nineteenth century and of the present.

I should like to quote a passage from a speech he gave in June of 1913 before the members of the France-Amérique Committee, in which Bergson tried to analyze the American ideal and expressed his admiration for those universities and colleges springing up in this country, as if brought forth by some volcanic eruption. In this simple and moving passage, he writes: "The main feature of the American soul is a certain idealism: by idealism I mean an ensemble of tendencies which are hard to define but which hardly need to be defined. First, curiosity for things of the mind, then the habit of placing the matters of the mind above all others. Finally and especially, I mean by idealism the habit of considering that life is not simply to be lived but that it has an objective and a 'raison d'être': . . . something must be achieved which does not yet exist, and when this 'something' is achieved it will make life richer and will give it a new significance."

This idealism is also very Bergsonian; it expresses the purest part of Bergson's philosophy which is essentially a philosophy of intimate freedom resulting from personal effort and creation. Here is a deep faith in the destiny of man, in the final triumph of light over darkness. There is no other meaning for Bergsonian "intuition."

by Jaroslav Pelikan

BERGSON AMONG THE THEOLOGIANS

In the history of theology, the philosopher has been cast in
the dual role of Don Juan and Simón Bolívar. He has appeared as a seducer and as a liberator. Ever since the New
Testament warning, "See to it that no one makes a prey of
you by philosophy and empty deceit" (Col. 2:8), philosophy has been seen as the seducer of theologians, enticing
them into thoughts and actions that violate their fidelity
to the Christian revelation. Less publicized perhaps, but
no less thoroughly documented in the history of theology,
is the role of the philosopher as liberator, delivering the
theologians from the onerous responsibility of making
their theologies conform to philosophical systems that are
passé and enabling the theologians to recognize issues and
implications in the Bible and in the traditions of the
Church that might have eluded them if they had not been
alerted by the philosophers. Of course, what one generation of theologians may regard as a liberation effected by
the philosophers may be interpreted by another generation
of theologians, or even by other theologians in their own

generation, as a seduction. Yet the history of theology does provide many illustrations of the liberating influence of the philosophers. It was Middle Stoicism that helped Tertullian to clarify the Christian notion of conscience, which is treated seminally but scantily in the New Testament.[1] It was the Aristotelian distinction of causes that was responsible for the deepening of the doctrine of creation among both Roman Catholic and Protestant theologians, who were alike indebted to Aristotle.[2] And it was thanks to Hegel that the Protestant theologians of the nineteenth century launched an era of historical study in theology unmatched by previous centuries.[3]

These and dozens of other instances in the history of theology are quite separable from the equally interesting question of how the history of religion and of theology may have helped to shape philosophy, from the Orphic elements in Plato to the Lutheran elements in Hegel. Thus there have been a few studies of the relation of Henri Bergson to the two religious traditions, Judaism and Roman Catholicism, that play their contrapuntal themes in his life and thought. The study of Bergson and Judaism by Aimé Pallière, brief though it is, suggests the complexity of his atti-

---

[1] Cf. J. H. Waszink, ed., *Quinti Septimi Florentis Tertulliani De Anima* (Amsterdam, 1947), for a detailed commentary upon the Greek and Christian elements in Tertullian's view of the soul.

[2] See James A. McWilliams, S.J., *Physics and Philosophy.* A study of Saint Thomas' Commentary on the Eight Books of Aristotle's Physics (Washington, 1945), pp. 106–9; Jaroslav Pelikan, *From Luther to Kierkegaard* (St. Louis, 1950), pp. 67, 74.

[3] Karl Barth, *Protestant Thought: From Rousseau to Ritschl,* introduction by Jaroslav Pelikan (New York, 1959), pp. 298–305.

tude toward the faith of his fathers. On the other hand, the more detailed examination of his ambivalence toward Roman Catholicism, published in 1941 by the philosopher-theologian Antonin Sertillanges, augmented by some material in the *Études bergsoniennes,* provides background for consideration of the apparent leanings toward the Church evident in Bergson's later years.[4] Neither of these books is as satisfying as their important subjects would demand, but they have at least made a beginning. From them we can see that in Bergson too the history of religion has had a part in the development of the history of philosophy.

This paper, however, is intended to show that in Bergson too the history of philosophy has had a part in the history of religion, and specifically in the history of theology. Clearly this part has not been as important as was the prestige of, let us say, Kant or Hegel a century ago, or of Kierkegaard in recent decades. Nevertheless, Bergson has been heard in the halls of the theologians, both as Don Juan and as Simón Bolívar. As could be expected, *The Two Sources of Morality and Religion* has received the most explicit consideration, but *Creative Evolution* has not been entirely overlooked for its possible contribution to the restatement of the Christian doctrine of God in relation to cosmogony. One of the most influential themes to come from Bergson is that indicated by the second and third chapters of *The Two Sources,* "static religion" and "dy-

[4] Antonin Sertillanges, *Bergson et le catholicisme* (Paris, 1941) ; Aimé Pallière, *Bergson et le judaisme* (Paris, 1933) ; Lydie Adolphe, *La philosophie religieuse de Bergson* (Paris, 1946).

namic religion." For the sake of formulating the issues as they have appeared in the history of theology, I shall speak of institution and intelligence as two phenomena in the religious life with which theologians have been obliged to come to terms. Both the idea of institution and the problem of intelligence have figured prominently in the history of Christian thought, but theologians have been embarrassed with each in turn; for they know that theology cannot avoid dealing with the problems of institution and intelligence, but that to deal with them adequately it must draw upon other resources than its own special materials of Scripture and tradition. Therefore these two problems have often been an obvious place to look beyond the theologian for the presence of the philosopher, cast as Don Juan or as Simón Bolívar or as both. My examination of Bergson's significance for the theological evaluation of institutions will be based upon the work of our contemporary, Professor H. Richard Niebuhr of Yale. My study of Bergson's significance for the theological understanding of intelligence will make use of the work of Bergson's contemporary, Alfred Loisy (1857–1940).

Christianity inherited the problem of institution from Judaism; but because it did not, and indeed could not, take over the institutions of Judaism, it has found the mere repetition of Old Testament answers to the problem impossible. Ironically, because Judaism regarded the institutional patterns of its communal life as the direct products of the special will of God, it could, in the prophetic tradition, be almost cavalier in its treatment of these patterns.

Christianity, on the other hand, may and sometimes does attribute its institutional structure to the explicit warrant of Jesus Christ himself; but even those theologians who make such an attribution recognize that the details of this institutional structure are not part of the original warrant, as they are in Judaism, but belong to the development of history, even though this development may be viewed as a special activity of God. Thus Christian theology has found the problem of institution as embarrassing as it is inevitable.[5]

Both the embarrassment and the inevitability became special problems for Protestant theology. Although the Reformers could speak as though institutions were expendable, they found themselves forced to create, adapt, and rationalize various institutions in order to carry out their reformatory work. When this embarrassment about institutions was combined with historical relativism, as it was at the end of the nineteenth and the beginning of the twentieth century, the result was a virtual identification of the institutional forms of the Church with Antichrist. For the cultivation of true Christian inwardness, the institution was a hindrance. Thus in the thought of Rudolph Sohm, the Church becomes a purely spiritual phenomenon; and the difference between Protestantism and Roman Catholicism is defined on the basis of their fundamental cleavage at this point.[6] The creation of institutionalized Christianity,

[5] Anders Nygren, *Christ and His Church*, translated by Alan Carlsten (Philadelphia, 1956), pp. 97–100.

[6] Rudolph Sohm, *Weltliches und geistliches Recht* (Munich and Leipzig, 1914), pp. 43–69.

with hierarchy and canon law, was the fall of the Church; the development of a Protestant hierarchy and a Protestant canon law was thus a relapse into Catholic institutionalism, and to this extent was a betrayal of the Reformation.

About the problem of institution in religion Bergson had much to say. The most memorable metaphor he employed was the definition of religion as "the crystallization, brought about by a scientific process of cooling, of what mysticism had poured, while hot, into the soul of man." [7] With this metaphor Bergson acknowledges the correct element in the notion of the fall of the Church. His whole contrast between "static religion" and "dynamic religion" rests upon the recognition that membership in a religious institution, however sacred its historical origin may be, cannot be equated with being religious; for by its very existence such an institution symbolizes the partial betrayal of the enthusiasm in which the religion originated. Bergson compared Christianity with Judaism at this point and identified nationalism, i.e., the confinement of religion to the confines of a single historical institution, as the reason for the replacement of Judaism by Christianity. He penetrated as few thinkers have into the conservatism of a religious institution: it can be so devoted to its own past that it is unable to recognize and to accept in the present a dynamic movement that is more loyal to the true past of the institution than the hierarchs are themselves. With the story of the Grand Inquisitor, Bergson shares the realiza-

[7] Henri Bergson, *The Two Sources of Morality and Religion*, translated by R. Ashley Audra and Cloudesley Brereton (Garden City, 1956), p. 238.

tion that Christ was not lynched by a ruffian mob, but cruci-
fied at the behest of institutionalized religion, which would
be willing to crucify Him again. Where this insight is lacking, religion degenerates into that observance of petty regulations and little pieties which Bergson describes with
such sharpness in his observations of conventional, institutional religion.

Still Bergson knows that saying this and no more than
this is irresponsible. Religious institutions may be a betrayal of high religion, but they are also its presupposition.
In the chapter on "static religion," building upon some of
the insights of Durkheim, he describes the necessity and
utility of religion as a defensive reaction aimed at social
survival.[8] To reject the institutions of religion out of hand
is to forget that they provide many with as much as they
are able to bear of genuine religious enthusiasm. The con-
cessions and compromises that mysticism is obliged to
make in order to gain acceptance are a high price, sometimes indeed too high a price. Yet the acceptance of an
institution may be the way to guard the possibility that
mysticism, or something like mysticism, may happen
again. Thus "mysticism and religion are mutually cause
and effect, and continue to interact on one another indefi-
nitely." [9] For this reason "mysticism is served by [institu-
tional] religion, against the day when religion becomes
enriched by his mysticism." [10] Indeed, "what the mystic
finds waiting for him . . . is a humanity which has been

---

[8] *Ibid.*, pp. 102 ff.; on Durkheim cf. pp. 104, 134, 184.
[9] *Two Sources*, p. 239.   [10] *Ibid.*

prepared to listen to his message by other mystics invisible and present in the religion which is actually taught." [11] For "religious dynamism needs static religion for its expression and diffusion." [12]

Both his historical observations and his philosophical consideration led Bergson to a sophisticated recognition of the needs and the limits of religious institutions. The reader should not be thrown off by Bergson's effort to restrict the term "religion" to its static, institutional expression. The term is not simply a pejorative for him, for it can mean "the adoration of the gods to whom men pray." [13] In this sense religion is a representation of that continuum to which mysticism, i.e., genuine and ultimate religion, leads and from which it also proceeds. Neither the identification of this ultimate with the rules of an institution nor a radical separation between the institution and the ultimate represents Bergson's mature judgment about the role of the institution in the history of religion. If I may be permitted to paraphrase this judgment in the language of traditional theology, Bergson seems to be saying that what we pray for is that the Kingdom of God might appear, if only briefly; but that while we are praying and waiting, we have to have the Church. This does not mean that the Church is the Kingdom, for it is not; but it does have a role in the coming of the Kingdom.

I have chosen these particular terms of traditional theology to paraphrase Bergson because H. Richard Niebuhr explicitly draws upon this very insight of Bergson in his

[11] *Ibid.*   [12] *Two Sources,* p. 179.   [13] *Ibid.,* p. 175.

important book on *The Kingdom of God in America,* and
then implicitly in his more recent books on *The Meaning
of Revelation* [14] and on *The Purpose of the Church and Its
Ministry.* I cannot presume to speak for Professor Niebuhr, who usually manages to speak very well for himself;
but it does seem to me that the problem of the relation between the Church and the Kingdom of God, that is, between institutionalized religion on the one hand, and what
Bergson calls "mysticism," on the other hand, is one of the
continuing issues to which Niebuhr has addressed himself
in his thought and research. Having learned from Ernst
Troeltsch to discern the social motives behind theological
rationalizations, Niebuhr devoted his volume on *The Social Sources of Denominationalism* to a careful examination of how social-political issues like slavery have been
more responsible for the denominational divisions in
American Protestantism than the ideological issues which
have provided the pretext for these divisions. [15]

When he came, therefore, to the description of *The
Kingdom of God in America,* Niebuhr needed an analysis
of the relation between religious faith and ecclesiastical institution that would do justice to his insight into the social
sources of denominationalism, but would at the same time
interpret the relation more dialectically than a one-sided
sociological interpretation could. This he found in Bergson. Quoting the very metaphor about crystallization and

[14] Cf. the prefatory remarks in H. Richard Niebuhr, *The Meaning of Revelation* (New York, 1941).

[15] H. Richard Niebuhr, *The Social Sources of Denominationalism* (New
York, 1957).

cooling to which I referred earlier, Niebuhr makes the observation: "The statement is subject to many criticisms, since it may be objected that the term 'religion' is as applicable to the dynamic process as it is to the crystallized product, that the process of cooling is not always scientific, that prophetism more than mysticism represents the dynamic element in Christianity, and that the molten fluid is poured into the social life rather than into individual souls. Nevertheless the philosopher of vitalism has described a process which had become unintelligible to modern men when it was set forth in the traditional terms of gospel and law, but which is a very real part of all religious life. The occasional crystallization or institutionalization of the kingdom of God movement is apparently inevitable." [16]

Although Niebuhr does not quote Bergson often in this book, he cites his authority at two crucial points: several times in the introductory chapter, which sets the terms and limits for his consideration of institutionalism and the Kingdom of God; and then again in the concluding chapter, which contains his evaluation of the patterns of institutionalization that have characterized American Protestantism. Thus the extent of Bergson's significance for Niebuhr could not be measured by a catalogue of the number of times he quotes *The Two Sources*. For the crucial problem of institution and *dynamis*, Bergson provides Niebuhr with an apparatus that is both critical and realistic. Just

[16] H. Richard Niebuhr, *The Kingdom of God in America* (New York, 1959), pp. 165–66.

this combination of the critical and the realistic is what
Niebuhr needed when, after surveying theological education in the United States and Canada, he proceeded to define *The Purpose of the Church and Its Ministry.* "We
need," he wrote, "to define Church further by use of the
polar terms 'community' and 'institution.' A social reality
such as the Church cannot be described by means of one
of these categories only and much misconception of the
Church results from such exclusive use. Popularly and
even among churchmen the institutional Church may be so
emphasized that there is little appreciation for the Church
that does not come to appearance in organizations and rites
. . . But the opposite error is also possible; a common
life, vaguely defined by reference to a common spirit also
vaguely described, is exalted at the expense of institutional forms." [17]

Now H. Richard Niebuhr was not the first to discover
this about the Church, nor was Henri Bergson. Nor, for
that matter, was Bergson Niebuhr's only mentor on this
question. Indeed, the impressive intellectual genealogy of
Niebuhr's thought compiled by his student and colleague,
Hans Frei, restricts itself almost entirely to the German
backgrounds of his theology. [18] In any case, it is essential to
note that the propositions and affirmations of the New
Testament by themselves would not suffice for the con-

[17] H. Richard Niebuhr, *The Purpose of the Church and Its Ministry* (New York, 1956), pp. 21–22.
[18] Hans W. Frei, "Niebuhr's Theological Background" in Paul Ramsey, ed., *Faith and Ethics.* The Theology of H. Richard Niebuhr (New York, 1957), pp. 9–64.

struction of such a doctrine of the Church. To discover this about the Church and to be freed from the necessity of choosing between form and matter or between institution and *dynamis*, a theologian needs a working theory about the validity and the limits of institutionalization; and he needs to get such a theory from those whose special calling it is to reflect upon this problem. For Niebuhr, then, Henri Bergson has been cast in the role of Simón Bolívar, delivering him both from the tyranny of a positivistic institutionalism and from the anarchy of a vacuous idealism. Bergson has helped him to realize that static religion is as inadequate as it is inevitable.

Bergson's interpretation of "dynamic religion" has likewise been significant in the history of modern theology, for it has enabled some modern theologians to come to terms with a problem as perennial and as perplexing as the problem of institution, namely, the problem of intelligence. The reconsideration of this problem in relation to myth, liturgy, science, and history was an assignment taken up by the movement in Roman Catholic theology labeled Modernism, whose outstanding French representative was Alfred Loisy. Denounced by Pope Pius X in 1907 as "the synthesis of all heresies," [19] the movement has nevertheless left its mark also upon orthodox Roman Catholic theologians. It agitated for the acceptance of historical-critical methods in the study of Scripture and dogma, but behind

[19] Pius X, *Pascendi dominici gregis*, September 8, 1907, in Henry Denzinger, ed., *The Sources of Catholic Dogma*, translated by Roy J. Deferrari (St. Louis, 1957), p. 539, no. 2105.

this lay an image of the role of the intelligence in religion that differed from the classical Roman Catholic image and came closer to Bergson's understanding.

I think it is fair to say that Bergson's insight into the relation between instinct, intuition, and intelligence in religion ranks among his most important contributions to theology. Defining the intelligence in its essence as the effort "to co-ordinate means with a view to a remote end, and to undertake what it does not feel absolutely sure of carrying out," [20] he saw that at its base religion could not be simply a matter of the intelligence, but preceded intelligence and provided it with some of the raw material for its reflection. This did not mean that the fundamental intuitions and instincts of religion and the practice of the intelligence were mutually exclusive; for, in Bergson's epigrammatic formula, "there still hangs around the edge of intelligence a fringe of instinct, and . . . in the depths of instinct there still survive gleams of intelligence." [21] On the other hand, it was a distortion of religion to interpret it as primarily an ideological system or a theology. Such an interpretation ascribed simultaneously too little and too much to religion.

Bergson pointed this out most clearly in his analysis of primitive religion. It amounted to an axiom for him: "We shall say it over and over again: before man can philosophize man must live; it is from a vital necessity that the primeval tendencies and convictions must have originated. To connect religion with a system of ideas, with a logic or a 'pre-logic,' is to turn our remote ancestors into intellec-

[20] *Two Sources*, p. 139.   [21] *Ibid.*, p. 118.

tuals, and intellectuals such as we ought to be in greatest numbers ourselves, for we often see the finest theories succumbing to passion and interest and holding good only in our hours of speculative thought, whereas ancient religions pervaded the whole of life." [22] This protest against the intellectualization of religion, so familiar to us from Søren Kierkegaard and Rudolf Otto, defended the essentials of religion against the reductionism so often urged by the intelligence. Among those essentials were two that are important for our purposes here—myth and ritual. Bergson's treatment of the myth-making function is free of the condescension with which so much of Western thought since the Enlightenment has discussed the early sagas of the world religions; Professor Manuel's recent study of Enlightenment arguments about myth reveals this contrast very sharply.[23] All this does not mean that Bergson was unaware of the deficiency in myth-making; he saw that it did not "clearly distinguish between the physical order and the moral or social order, between intentional orderliness due to the obedience of all to a law and the orderliness manifested in the course of nature." [24] Still he was able to treat myth with genuine and profound understanding as one of man's cardinal efforts to give meaning to life.

Less prominent than myth in Bergson's interpretation, but present nonetheless, was ritual. Modern study of the history of religion, including and especially the history of Israel and of primitive Christianity, has stressed the close

[22] *Ibid.*, p. 176.
[23] Frank E. Manuel, *The Eighteenth Century Confronts the Gods* (Cambridge, Mass., 1959).
[24] *Two Sources*, p. 124.

connection between myth and ritual as basic components of religion.[25] Bergson's study of the history of religion had provided him with examples of the prominence of ritual, and he stressed this against the intellectualization of the relation behind ritual action. "It would be an error," he argues, "to regard as an abstract idea—I mean an idea extracted from things by an intellectual effort—the representation of the act and of its continuation . . . We cannot too often repeat that the action may be forthcoming first and be self-sufficient." [26] "There is," he summarized, "no religion without rites and ceremonies. The religious representation is above all an occasion for these religious acts. They doubtless emanate from belief, but they at once react on it and strengthen it: if gods exist, they must have their worship; but since there is worship, then there must be gods." [27] Therefore Bergson insisted that it is wrong to assign to the intelligence functions that actually belong to the myths and rituals by which primitive religion seeks to provide men and societies with protection and reassurance against the imminent prospect of their own dissolution.

Nor is it only in primitive religion that intelligence has a limited function. The history of so-called "high religion" is also unintelligible without a realistic assessment of what ideas can and cannot do.[28] A comparison of Stoic and Christian proclamations about universal brotherhood re-

[25] Joachim Wach, *The Comparative Study of Religions*, introduction by Joseph M. Kitagawa (New York, 1958), pp. 97–120.
[26] *Two Sources*, p. 180.   [27] *Ibid.*, p. 201.
[28] Cf. Friedrich Heiler, *Prayer. A Study in the History and Psychology of Religion*, translated by Samuel McComb (New York, 1958), pp. xv–xvi.

vealed to Bergson, for example, that "the words were almost the same; but they did not find the same echo, because they were not spoken with the same accent. The Stoics provided some very fine examples. If they did not succeed in drawing humanity after them, it is because Stoicism is essentially a philosophy. The philosopher who is so enamoured of this noble doctrine as to become wrapped up in it doubtless vitalizes it by translating it into practice; just so did Pygmalion's love breathe life into the statue once it was carven. But it is a far cry from that to the enthusiasm which spreads from soul to soul, unceasingly, like a conflagration. Such an emotion may indeed develop into ideas which make up a doctrine, or even several different doctrines having no other resemblance between them than a kinship of the spirit; but it precedes the idea instead of following it." [29] I have quoted this remarkable passage at length because it so well summarizes Bergson's programme for religion, as well as the interpretation of the role of intelligence that Loisy and his colleagues sought to establish (or, as they claimed, re-establish) in the Church.

Although Loisy was primarily an historian of Christianity and an exegete of the New Testament, he felt obliged, upon the publication of Bergson's *The Two Sources*, to write a full-length reply.[30] A study of Loisy's argumentation in this little-known work discloses that

[29] *Two Sources*, pp. 60–61.

[30] Alfred Loisy, *Y a-t-il deux sources de la religion et de la morale?* (2nd ed.; Paris, 1934).

much in Bergson's position squared with his own interpretations of religion and morality, but that at several decisive points he found the position unsatisfactory. Perhaps the most decisive of these unsatisfactory points was Bergson's designation of Christ and the apostles as mystics. According to Bergson, "if the great mystics are indeed such as we have described them, they are the imitators, and original but incomplete continuators, of what the Christ of the Gospels was completely." [31] To this Loisy objects on the grounds that a study of the New Testament does not substantiate such a picture of the religion of Jesus, nor an interpretation of St. Paul that would put him so unequivocally into the succession of the "true mystics." [32] He therefore accuses Bergson of imposing his own conception of the "true mystic" upon the picture of Christ in the Gospels.

Nevertheless, this basic disagreement with Bergson, which occupies a major part of Loisy's book, must not be permitted to obscure their even more basic agreement at the very points I have stressed. Speaking from his study of the history of non-Christian religions and from his work as a New Testament scholar, Loisy finds himself obliged to agree with much of what Bergson says about the role of myth and ritual in religion, also in Christianity.[33] Religion is not in the first place a set of ideas, but an intuition about life, expressed in the form of myth and ritual; in this Loisy and Bergson concur. What Loisy adds to Bergson is a somewhat more ample consideration of the place

---

[31] Bergson, *Two Sources*, p. 240.
[32] Loisy, *Y a-t-il deux sources?*, pp. 43, 144 ff.   [33] *Ibid.*, pp. 136 ff.

that ritual occupies alongside myth in the evolution of religion.[34] This applies both to the sacrifices of the world
religions, especially of the primitive religions, and to the
sacraments of Christianity. Therefore, theology must be
liturgical theology. Here Loisy's empirical historical study
permits him to amplify Bergson. But this merely reinforces
their basic agreement that doctrines do not build religion,
but religion (understood as the myth and ritual of a society) builds doctrines. The role of intelligence is to reflect
upon this and thus, in relation to the destruction that
threatens nature, "to set up intelligence against intelligence. The intellectual representation which thus restores
the balance to nature's advantage is of a *religious* order." [35]
Theology and dogma do not generate the substance, but
preserve the form of devotion; this they do by their abstract teachings. Bergson is willing to raise the question "if
these abstract teachings are not at the root of mysticism,
and if the latter has ever done more than go over the letter
of dogma, in order to retrace it in characters of flame." [36]
But finally both Bergson and Loisy assign to dogma a subsidiary role in the true life of the spirit.

In Loisy's case as much as in Niebuhr's, loose talk about
"influence" is undoubtedly out of place. But it is in place
to point out that this insight into the relatively subsidiary
role of intelligence, i.e., of dogma and theology, in the religious life has become a self-evident presupposition for
historians of Christianity as well as for historians of the
non-Christian religions. *Lex orandi lex credendi* is now a

[34] *Ibid.*, pp. 73 ff.   [35] Bergson, *Two Sources*, p. 129.   [36] *Ibid.*, p. 36.

basic axiom of theological research. Bergson was certainly
only one of the thinkers and scholars of the past century
who came to this insight and transmitted it to the theologians. The importance of Bergson was partly his effort to
combine this insight with his concept of emergence—an
effort with which, it seems to me, theologians have not yet
come to terms. But he did help the theologians to come to
terms with the materials of their own field more adequately
than they had before, as the examples of both H. Richard
Niebuhr and Alfred Loisy illustrate.

It was, then, as Simón Bolívar that Henri Bergson acted
in the thought of both these Christian theologians. Neither
the theological meaning of the institution nor the religious
significance of the intelligence can be evaded by the
thoughtful theologian, and neither of these problems can
be handled by means of theological sources alone. If the
theologian cannot avoid them and if he cannot handle them
purely as a theologian, he must go elsewhere for help. He
must turn to a Simón Bolívar for liberation, even though
he always runs the danger that Don Juan will come along
for the fun of it. The significance of Bergson for these two
theologians thus provides a useful case-study for consideration of the problem of theology and philosophy. Although
Paul Tillich says that philosophy raises questions and theology gives answers, in these cases at least the situation is
reversed. The questions are raised by the history of theology within the context of the history of the Church, and the
answers cannot come from theology itself but must be provided by a more generalized reflection about the nature of

institution and of intelligence. Thus philosophy helps the theologians to be better theologians. I do not believe that this has always been the case, but I do believe that philosophy has performed this role often enough to make it worth hearing. I believe further that theology has not yet heard the last of Henri Bergson. He deserves to be heard again, at least for another hundred years.

by Enid Starkie

BERGSON AND LITERATURE

I feel that what follows deserves an apology. I am not a trained philosopher, and I do not even know Bergson's work very well. I do not think that I would even go so far as to claim that I understand all his ideas. I know that I am not here talking about him as a philosopher, but it is, I feel, as well to understand the philosophy of an author whom one is discussing. When I was young I was much moved by some of his writings—especially by *Creative Evolution* and the treatise on laughter; and later by *Morality and Religion*—but I think that it was probably his style, his form of imagery, which moved me, and I believe that my experience was a literary rather than an intellectual pleasure. Bergson wrote one of the most melodious and harmonious styles of his time which was a joy to read, and there are passages concerning literature in *Laughter* which are amongst the most perceptive that I have ever read. He was in tune with the spiritual and Symbolist literature which was my favourite reading then—and even now—and I felt that I could see with his eyes.

I was not unique in this; it was the experience of all
those who thronged his lectures at the Collège de France
between 1900 and 1921, when he retired. This was before
my time, and I never heard him personally, though he was
to die in 1941 at the age of eighty-two. But, later when I
was a student in Paris, I knew many who had gone earlier
to his courses, and who all described the wonder and the
magic of the experience.

To understand Bergson's significance he should not be
considered only as a philosopher. He was certainly not of
the same philosophic family as—for instance—Aristotle,
Descartes or Kant. It is indeed fashionable today amongst
philosophers to denigrate his contribution to philosophy,
and to deny him the name of philosopher at all. One must
also take into account the period in which he flourished in
the history of thought in France, and the feeling of liberation which he gave to many people, the feeling of hope in a
better world of thought. He gave that hope with authority
because he was a trained philosopher, and not merely an
aesthete waffling sentimentally. He gave hope to those who
were not philosophers just because he was a thinker himself who used his mind. And, by making up the quarrel
between the idealists and realists, he set spiritual values
again on the map, on a firm basis of intellectual experience.
He considered that, in the academic teaching of his youth,
intuition had been sacrificed to the intellect, and yet he
believed that intuition alone could reveal the unity of life,
that if a unity existed, it must be a spiritual one, that life
must be wider than the intellect and the materiality which

binds us. Bergson's ideas lit up the path for many other minds which had been wandering in a wilderness.

One must remember what was the state of intellectual studies in the university when Bergson began to teach, in order to appreciate the force of his message, and to give it full justice. This was the time when Hyppolite Taine's theries were the staple intellectual diet. Their main feature was a passionate and intolerant cult of positive science, so that metaphysics was considered only a deception or an empty fantasy. The dream of thinkers was the discovery of a universal science, a mathematics which would explain everything, and this was expected to fulfill all the needs of man. Everything was subjected to it and explained by it. Taine, in the introduction to his history of English literature, declared that vice and virtue did not exist as moral factors but were only two products like vitriol and sugar, neither of which was better than the other, only dissimilar to it. He even considered that the whole of art and literature could be explained rationally, by scientific investigation, through the principle of Race, Environment and Historical Moment. That is to say that it would be stated scientifically, and inevitably, what kind of art would be produced by any given people at a given moment of history, and in a given environment. This theory left completely out of account personal genius, and, like psychoanalysis, it could not be concerned with aesthetic or spiritual values.

But, after the Franco-Prussian War, especially from the eighteen-eighties onwards, there was growing dissatisfaction with rationalism and positivism, with the amoral and unspiritual attitude of Taine's teaching, and this is seen clearly in the novel by Paul Bourget, *The Disciple*, published in 1889. The hero is a young man who has always taken to heart the teaching of his Master, who, in his magnum opus, *The Anatomy of Will*, expressed the theory that all human desires follow certain inevitable laws; and that crime and virtue only exist from the social point of view but that, for the philosopher, they are meaningless.

The young man seduces a young girl who is engaged to another man, and then promises her that they will commit suicide together, but he backs out of the pact and she dies alone. He writes to his Master, in despair, for help and comfort, saying:

I write to you *de profundis*. Answer me, dear Master, I implore you, direct me, guide me! Strengthen me in the doctrine which was, and still is, mine; in the conviction of universal necessity, which means that our worst actions—this cold plan of seduction, the suicide pact—all are part of the natural laws of the immense universe. Tell me that I'm not a monster, that there are no monsters; that you'll still be there, if I escape this terrible ordeal, and that you'll accept me again as a disciple.

The old professor is filled with horror when he discovers the results of his teaching. After the girl's fiancé kills the young man, and when he himself watches beside the bed where his young follower lies ready for burial, he is overcome with horror and remorse at the outcome of his life's work.

During the night which followed this tragic scene, the admirers of *The Anatomy of Will* would have been astonished if they

could have read what was going on in the mind of their venerable
Master. At the foot of the bed where the dead man lay, the mother
knelt praying and, seated on a chair, the great "negator" was
watching the woman pray and, for the first time in his life, felt
his thought not strong enough to uphold him; this analyst, who
was almost inhuman through logic, was humbling himself and
prostrating himself before the impenetrable mystery of human
destiny. The words of the only prayer which he still remembered
from his far-distant childhood, rose to his mind: "Our Father
who art in Heaven!" He did not, in fact, pronounce them, and
perhaps would never do so again, but they were the only words
which occurred to him to meet the situation.

In the Symbolist movement in French literature there
had also been a reaction against positivism and materialism. The writers had found their theories largely in Baudelaire, who had been, during the Second Empire, the only
poet in France to have spiritual aspirations and not to be
wedded to positivism, but he was not understood or ap-
preciated in his own day.

Baudelaire had seen art as an essentially spiritual activity, its main function being to get into touch with the
beyond, with the ideal. For him there was a unity in art,
and he dreamed of one perfect art encompassing all the
rest, and appealing to all the senses in one. This could not,
however, be achieved through the efforts of reason alone.
Indeed the only way to reach it was to break down the
tyranny of the mind by any possible means. Later Rimbaud was to say that the poet could reach the ultimate only
through the "dérèglement de tous les sens," by becoming a

sensitive plate on which impressions could be written without his volition or effort. The poet was to become an inspired prophet or seer, through which the eternal voice
found expression.

Later on, in 1934, Daniel-Rops was to declare that any
action which tended to ruin the primacy of reason, to hu-
miliate it for the part it dares to play on earth, seemed to
him worthy of interest.

Bergson, who was in his middle twenties when the Symbolist movement began, is nearer in thought to these writers
than to the academic philosophers of his time, and he was
either influenced by them, or else the products of his mind
sprang up from the same roots and needs, in the same soil.
He became for them the heaven-sent thinker, who carried
their theories further, who had the authority of a trained
mind, and who was not merely a sentimental and emotional
aesthetician, such as Villiers de L'Isle Adam and Théodore
de Wyzewa. He became the link between the men of letters
of the literary coteries and the men of scholarship of the
learned academies.

Many of the younger students at the Sorbonne at this
time were disillusioned and dissatisfied with the intellectual fare which they were being offered by their teachers,
and they felt that the spiritual side of their nature was
being starved. The University was then so hermetically
sealed within itself that any hope of change, any chance of
resurrection or renaissance, seemed impossible. Young
Jacques Maritain and Raïssa, whom he had just married,
were students at the Sorbonne at the beginning of the new

century. She tells us in her autobiography, written after she escaped from France, during the late war, *We have Been Young Together* (published in New York in 1942), of their despair and hopelessness at the aridity of their lives and beliefs. She describes what she calls their "unhappy and cruel universe, wherein the sole light was the philosophy of skepticism and relativism."

Finally, in despair at the vanity of their present and future, the young couple decided that, for a little while longer they would bear with existence, treating it like an experiment, in the hope that life would reveal itself, that some new values would stand forth so clearly as to enlist their total allegiance, and deliver them from the nightmare of a sinister and useless world. Then, if the experiment should prove unsuccessful, they would envisage their only solution in suicide, in a deliberate and reasonable suicide, before the years had accumulated their dust, before their youthful strength was completely spent. Then they would die of their own free will, of their own free choice, if it was not possible to live according to some spiritual truth. At the Sorbonne they had been given nothing but dust and ashes by their teachers, the pseudoscientific skepticism and relativeness which did violence to that idea of truth of which Pascal speaks. They wanted something else.

Their disillusionment had been complete when, suddenly, one day, they went to the Collège de France to hear one of Bergson's lectures. Raïssa Maritain declared that it was God's infinite mercy which caused her and her husband to find Henri Bergson in their great spiritual distress.

At that time Bergson had just arrived at the Collège de France, whose buildings lie across the rue Saint Jacques from the Sorbonne, but it was much further than that stretch of street in thought, and it was an adventurous step which the Maritains took when they crossed it. A mountain of prejudice separated the two institutions—particularly on the side of the Sorbonne, for whom Bergson was anathema. The feeling was so strong, says Raïssa Maritain, that it was as hard to go from the Sorbonne to the Collège de France, as from the Sorbonne to the Church of Saint Étienne du Mont at the top of the street.

The pilot who guided them across that dangerous straight was Charles Péguy, the declared enemy of the Sorbonne, who had the offices of his paper, *Les Cahiers de la Quinzaine,* across the street from the Sorbonne, in the rue de la Sorbonne.

There had been in Jacques and Raïssa Maritain, since childhood, an overpowering feeling for truth, as it were a door ajar on the road of life, but, until the unforgettable day when they first heard Bergson speak, this idea of truth, this hope of suspected discoveries had been explicitly and implicitly frustrated by all those from whom they had hoped to gain light. Then they heard Bergson and immediately were transported into another world and, thanks to him, their minds were cleansed of the scientific superstitions on which they had been nourished at the Sorbonne.

The great hall at the Collège de France in which Bergson lectured was too small to hold all those who wanted to hear him speak, and were eager to receive his message. The largest number of them were not philosophers, many were—as Tancrède de Visan said in an article in *Excelsior* on 14 February, 1914—fashionable ladies who sent their grooms to keep places for them, and they asked for a larger hall so as to be more comfortably seated. Amongst the auditors was Ernest Psichari, the grandson of the notorious free-thinker, Renan; this was the Ernest Psichari whose *Voyage du Centurion* marks one of the first steps in the Catholic revival in France. There were also the future art critic, Henri Focillon, the poet Anna de Noailles, the future Catholic writers, Charles Péguy, and Jacques and Raïssa Maritain, and the future Existentialist philosopher, Jean Wahl. Péguy and Psichari were both to be killed in the 1914 war. Maritain was later to talk of his passionate devotion to Bergson in his youth, to whom he owed his delivery from the idols of materialism. And Bergson was to declare that Maritain was the one of his students who had best understood and interpreted his thought. In a sense it was the philosopher who led Maritain, and many others, back to the faith. Raïssa Maritain says that the consummate art with which Bergson expounded his views, and his inspired sincerity, seemed to carry them along in the development of his discoveries, but in no way diminished the subtlety or technical perfection of his teaching.

To those unhappy young people who were lost in a wilderness of doubt and rationalism, to Péguy, Psichari, Jacques and Raïssa Maritain, to all of them, through Bergson's inspiration, spiritual perspectives of intellectual certainty were again beginning to open up. As Raïssa says, she felt as if she had "rediscovered the light-heartedness of childhood through his teaching." They had gone to the Collège de France, with an overwhelming anxiety and a sincere expectation, but they had returned, as she describes it, "carrying our little bouquets of truth and promises, as though vitalised by healthful air—prolonging to greater and still greater lengths our conversations on the Master's teaching. Winter was passing and spring was coming."

All of them arrived nearly an hour ahead of time to be sure of getting in, for many were turned away each day at the door.

Bergson's teaching, in its positive aspects, supplied his hearers with the possibility of metaphysical work, and unmasked the sophisms on which the mechanistic and materialistic theories of the day were founded, sweeping from the philosophical terrain a great number of pseudo problems or false solutions.

The teachers at the Sorbonne had made light of moral problems; they had scorned religious experience, denied freedom and made idealism impossible. What is called the soul was reduced to the body; psychology was replaced by physiology; while evolutionary doctrine had been turned into a heartless assertion of natural selection, the struggle for life, and the survival of the fittest. Bergson reversed all this, and brought back poetry and mystic intuition. He vindicated freedom and idealism, and freed the stream of consciousness. He challenged the materialists, and made the vital force a spiritual impulse, a freeing of the mind from matter and insisting on its creative powers. He saw spiritual energy existing as a concrete force of the soul.

At this time when these young people were attending Bergson's lectures, he was composing his *Creative Evolution,* and they got the theories from him, red-hot from the anvil, before they had had time to solidify. This was the science of spiritual impulse and impetus, to lay the foundations of mysticism. He considered that our civilization, our science, our intellect were all too materialistic and they must return to spirituality, though the task would not be an easy one. Humanity, he declared, cannot live by machinery, for it needs metaphysics. It was important to make an appeal to the whole of man, to allow man to follow his own inspiration, and for him to act according to his complete self. That was part also of the teaching of André Gide. All this could only be achieved, he thought, through intuition. Intuition was, as he said, "a lamp almost extinguished, which only glimmers wherever a vital interest is at stake. On our personality, our liberty, on the place we occupy in the whole of nature, on our destiny, it throws only a feeble and vacillating light, but which, nevertheless, pierces the darkness of the night in which our intellect leaves us."

The young people felt that Bergson had restored metaphysics to its proper place, and he was able to assure them that they would be able to know reality, that through intuition they would be able to attain the absolute and "know what is."

It was natural that Bergson should be attracted by the mystical theories of Symbolism, away from the French rationalism of the day, for he had not a drop of French blood in his veins, and the Symbolist Movement was one of international feeling. Its most advanced literature was not specifically French—indeed, many of the writers were foreigners, like Jean Moréas, Stuart Merril and Vielé-Griffin.

His father came from a Polish-Jewish family, while his mother was Irish. He was educated in France and, eventually, became a naturalized Frenchman. Like most of his French contemporaries, he started by being a rationalist, but, while teaching at Clermont-Ferrand, the home of Pascal, he turned against materialism. At that time he also came under the influence of the philosopher Émile Boutroux, who had started as a Kantian, but then discovered that his reason did not get him very far. Boutroux was probably the first philosopher to question scientific rationalism, and he followed Pascal in believing that the heart has its reasons which reason does not know. "Le coeur a ses raisons que la raison ne connaît pas." In his book on Pascal, which Bergson was to read with great interest, he turned towards metaphysics, and fought against the theory of the world as pure reason.

Bergson, in his doctoral thesis entitled *Time and Free-Will*, published in 1889—the same year as Bourget's *The Disciple*—already asserted the freedom of the mind as an experimental fact, to be realized by intuition. This was very daring at the time. He wanted, he said, to build up again the bridge between metaphysics and science, which had been demolished since Kant.

In his next book, *Matter and Memory*, Bergson showed

that he believed that the mind could have some effect on matter in a mysterious way. He thought that intellectual knowledge does not give reality as it is, but transmutes it into a set of symbols which are useful for the guidance of action, but which have no metaphysical significance. By symbols here he does not mean the symbols of the Symbolists, but only such symbols as telegraphic signs. He believed that if philosophy was to become a true metaphysics it must relinquish the method of analysis for that of intuition. The mind must place itself into a living relation with its object; it must, for the time being, become the object itself, through the exercise of intellectual sympathy. Only then will it be able to follow the creative movement and to grasp its living wholeness, instead of seeing it as so many separate things and states.

In *Morality and Religion* he writes:

A work of genius is in most cases the outcome of an emotion, unique of its kind, which seemed to baffle expression, and yet *had* to express itself. But is not this so of all work, however imperfect, into which there enters some degree of creativeness? Anyone engaged in writing has been in a position to feel the difference between an intelligence left to itself and that which burns with the fire of an original and unique emotion, born of the identification of the author with his subject, that is to say of intuition. In the first case the mind cold-hammers the materials, combining together ideas long since cast into words and which society supplies in a solid form. In the second it would seem that the solid materials supplied by intelligence first melt and mix, then solidify into fresh ideas now shaped by the creative mind itself . . . But it is in such a case only that the mind feels itself, or believes itself, to be creative. It no longer starts from a multiplicity of ready-made elements to arrive at a composite unity. It has been transported at a bound to something which seems both one and unique . . . Unique of its kind, it has sprung up in the soul of a poet and there alone, before stirring our own; and from this emotion the work has sprung, to this emotion the author was continually harking back throughout the composition of the work. It was no more than a creative exigency, but it was a specific one, now satisfied once the work is finished, which would not have been satisfied by any other work.

In the *Introduction to Metaphysics* he said that the absolute can only be reached and expressed through intuition, and by this he meant the spiritual sympathy by which one places oneself within an object in order to coincide with what is unique in it, and consequently inexpressible. Analysis, on the contrary, is the operation which reduces it to elements common to it and to other objects. He therefore considered that there were two types of knowledge: intellectual and intuitive—the intellectual being directed towards the already known, and the intuitive attaching itself to the unknown, the being-made. The intellect, according to him, is totally incapable of grasping time, motion, and life, while these are the unique objects of intuition.

Philosophers who are in disagreement with Bergson believe that if the intuitive method which he advocated were adopted instead of their critical method of reflection, then philosophy would be condemned to remain forever silent and inarticulate; or if philosophy sought to express itself it could do so only through Symbolism, which is literature and not philosophy. This was, however, the belief of Baudelaire and the Symbolists, that the deep reality, the absolute, which we perceive in a state of vision, can never be expressed directly in logical words, but can only be communicated through symbols.

In *Laughter* Bergson has written a passage which expresses this very clearly:

What is the object of art? Could reality come into direct contact with sense and consciousness, could we enter into immediate communion with things and with ourselves, probably art would be useless, or rather we should all be artists, for then our soul would continually vibrate in perfect accord with nature. Our eyes, aided by memory, would carve out in space and fix in time the most inimitable pictures. Deep in our souls we should hear the strains of our inner life's unbroken melody—a music that is ofttimes gay, but more frequently plaintive and always original. All this is around us and within us, and yet no whit of it do we perceive distinctly. Between nature and ourselves, nay between ourselves and our own consciousness a veil is interposed; a veil that is dense and opaque for the common herd,—thin, almost transparent, for the artist and the poet . . . So art, whether it be painting or sculpture, poetry or music, has no other object than to brush aside the utilitarian symbols, the conventional and socially accepted generalities, in short, everything that veils reality from us, in order to bring us face to face with reality itself. It is from a misunderstanding on this point that the dispute between realism and idealism in art has arisen . . . We might say, without in any way playing upon the meaning of words, that realism is in the work when idealism is in the soul, that it is only through ideality that we can resume contact with reality.

That is also the method of Proust, which he expounds in the last volume of his work, *The Past Recaptured:*

I felt there might be underneath these signs something quite different which I ought to try to discover, a thought which they transcribed after the manner of those hieroglyphics which one might think represented only material objects. Most assuredly this deciphering was difficult but it alone offered some truth to be read. For the truths that the intelligence grasps directly and openly in the full lighted world are somehow less profound, less indispensable than those which life has communicated to us without our knowledge through the form of impressions, material because they have come through our senses, but the inner meaning of which we can discern . . . I must try to interpret the sensations as indications of corresponding laws and ideas; I must try to think, that is to say, bring out of the obscurity what I had felt, and convert it into a spiritual equivalent. Now this method which seemed to me the only one, what was it other than to create a work of art.

This is also what André Gide writes, in his "Traité du Narcisse" (The "Treatise of Narcissus"), which contains one of the best definitions of the ideals of Symbolism:

Appearances are imperfect, they only half reveal the truth which they conceal; the poet must be able, at a hint, to understand these truths, and then to reveal them . . . The poet who knows that he is creating, divines behind each object—and one only suffices him—symbols, to reveal its archetype; he knows that appearance is only a pretext, a garment which hides it, and beyond which the gaze of the common herd does not penetrate, but which indicates that it is there. The poet contemplates these symbols, piously leaning over them, and then, silently, penetrates into the heart of the matter. And when, visionary, he has perceived the Idea, the harmonious Number of his being, which sustains the imperfect form, he seizes it, then, regardless of the transitory shape which clothed it in time, he knows how to give it its eternal shape, its true form, final and inevitable, heavenly and crystal-clear.

Bergson considered that his predecessors, when they had not despised intuition, had elevated it too far above the world, had isolated it from everything. He wanted to give it a scientific basis. He saw man as being made up of both intellect and intuition. Intellect could give only a very relative and practical idea of objects. But intuition enables us to enter into the object itself. Within all of us is a spiritual power in which we can take refuge and meditate. It is there that are found the deep roots of our personality, communicating with all nature. Like his inspirer Pascal, he believed in truth directly revealed to the heart. True intuition, he says, "by a kind of intellectual auscultation is able to feel the throbbing of its soul"; it is able to attain the absolute. That is mysticism. In *Morality and Religion,* he writes of mystic experience:

True mystics simply open their souls to the oncoming wave. Sure of themselves, because they feel within them something better than themselves, they prove to be greater men of action, to the surprise of those for whom mysticism is nothing but visions, and raptures, and ecstasies. That which they have allowed to flow into them is a stream flowing down and seeking through them to reach their fellowmen; the necessity to spread about them what they have received affects them like the onslaught of love. A love which each one of them stamps with his own personality. A love which is in each of them an entirely new emotion, capable of transposing human life into another tone.

Bergson thought that the divorce between science and metaphysics was the greatest evil from which modern philosophy suffers. In his *Introduction to Metaphysics,* he declared that "concepts are only symbols"—meaning only hieroglyphics—"substituted for the images which they symbolise, and which are incapable of giving more than an artificial reconstruction of the subject; they present the shadow of reality." He believed that there was something in the universe which science cannot weigh, measure, or calculate, and which it will never be able to calculate. But a true intuitive philosophy would be able to realize the much desired union between science and metaphysics.

Bergson's spiritual attitude to philosophy influenced the Catholic revival in the twentieth century, such writers as l'Abbé Brémond, Charles du Bos, Charles Péguy, Paul Claudel, Julien Green—and many others. Raïssa Maritain says that Bergson had created in them all an enthusiasm and a joyous gratitude, which was to last them for many years, even through grave philosophical differences and despite necessary and sustained criticism.

As he grew older, Bergson was moving closer to religion, to Christianity. In 1920, in his *Spiritual Energy,* he began to consider the possibility of the human soul. The consideration received fuller expression in his *Morality and Religion,* published in 1932. This effected the fusion of Christianity and philosophy, though he never became a

Catholic himself—he did not wish to do so while his people, the Jews, were being persecuted. As Raïssa Maritain
said: "Bergson travelled uncertainly towards God, still far
off, but the light of whom had already reached him, and us
through him."

No philosopher in France—with the exception of Descartes, perhaps, who must be studied in order to understand the seventeenth century—was better entitled than
Bergson to be studied, amongst the men of letters, as an
integral part of the literature. He was read not only by philosophers, but by all men of letters, and he spoke the kind
of language which all understood. His lectures at the Collège de France were a social event. They were thronged
with people from all sections and classes of the community. With philosophers, scientists, men of letters, students,
priests, clergymen, rabbis, and fashionable women, holding their finger tips together, high up before him, to show
that they were clapping silently, since applause at lectures
was not the custom. It was very "snob" to go to hear him
lecture, and he harmonized well with the literary and artistic trends of the day.

His approach to his work was literary and artistic more
than intellectual—he must have inherited this creative tal-
ent from his father who had been something of a musician.
Bergson saw the clearest evidence of intuition in the work
of the artist. It is the same conception which we find in
Baudelaire's poem, *Les Phares*, where each artist is seen
as a beacon shining in the surrounding darkness to light it
up, and also to show God that man is there.

> They are a cry passed on by a thousand sentinels,
> An order re-echoed through a thousand megaphones;
> They are a beacon lighted on a thousand citadels,
> A call from hunters lost deep in the woods.

Genius, Bergson believed, was the power the artist possessed of seeing more than ordinary people can, of enabling him, by his superior experience and intuition, to penetrate further into reality. Writing about the philosopher Ravaisson, he said that from the contemplation of a work of art could arise more concentrated truth than can be found in a philosophic treatise. He himself was first and foremost an artist, and a great many of his most telling efforts came from the beauty and harmony of his style. As a poet, ideas did not seem to exist for him until they had crystallized in an image. He was a poet in language—we see that in his use of metaphor. In his *Introduction to Metaphysics*, he says: "Is it astonishing that, like children trying to catch smoke by closing their hands, philosophers so often see the object they would grasp fly away before them?" This is a literary image rather than a philosophic concept. He was a poet with a beautifully modulated voice. Those with this gift of the tongue have always given the impression of visionary powers. It was thus also with Mallarmé at his Tuesday evening literary sessions at the rue de Rome. Bergson's lectures awakened in his hearers a sense of mystery through the imagination, and it seemed to reach to the core of their being, where the springs of consciousness well up. Like the Symbolist poets he managed to suggest a spiritual reality which he had perceived himself. People listened to the beauty of the style and not all paused to think whether there was any profound meaning contained in it. The passage which ends *Laughter* is very typical of such speaking—or writing:

Such is also the truceless warfare of the waves on the surface of the sea, whilst profound peace reigns in the depths below. The billows clash and collide with each other, as they strive to find their level. A fringe of snow-white foam, feathery and frolicsome, follows their changing outlines. From time to time the receding wave leaves behind a remnant of foam on the sandy beach. The child who plays hard by, picks up a handful, and, the next moment, is astonished to find that nothing remains in his grasp but a few drops of water, water that is far more brackish, far more bitter, than that of the waves which brought it. Laughter comes into being in the self-same fashion. It indicates a slight revolt on the surface of social life. It instantly adopts the changing forms of the disturbance. It, also, is a froth with a saline base. Like froth it sparkles. It is gaiety itself. But the philosopher who gathers a handful to taste may find that the substance is scanty, and the after-taste bitter.

Bergson's eloquent and precise language held his audience enthralled, so that no distraction was possible. The attention of his listeners did not wander for a moment, nothing could break the precious thread of the discourse. It was like perfect and beautiful music, captivating the mind, just as music's richness does, allowing it no escape. The absence of heavy technical vocabulary made it all a joy to hear, and he was the least Germanic of philosophers. His words slipped out as if on silk, and the rhythm lulled the senses of his hearers so that they felt that they saw with his eyes, with the eyes of a poet. Indeed, in his *Introduction to Metaphysics* he frequently compares the philosopher and the poet. And yet he had a profound distrust of language, that is logical language, which he felt to be too abstract. Like the Symbolists he believed that there were thoughts so profound that words were powerless to express them, that abstraction created a veil which hides reality from us. Music he felt was more capable of being a satisfactory art, as it was dynamic, the very manifestation of the activity which pushes the world forward, its vibrations laden with our emotions which enable us to recover contact with life. Talking of musical experience, in *Morality and Religion,* he said:

We feel, while we listen, as though we could not desire anything else but what the music is suggesting to us, and that that is just as we should naturally and necessarily act did we not refrain from action to listen. Let the music express joy or grief, pity or love, every moment we are what it expresses. Not only ourselves, but many others, nay, all the others, too. When music weeps, all humanity, all nature, weeps with it. In point of fact it does not introduce these feelings into us, it introduces us into them, as passers-by are forced into a street dance. Thus do pioneers in morality proceed. Life holds for them unsuspected tones of feeling like those of some new symphony, and they draw us after them into this music that we may express it in action.

Bergson had a clear understanding of artistic creation, and he was able to draw illustrations from it. He says:

Anyone who has attempted literary composition, knows that when the subject has been studied at length, the materials are all collected, and the notes all made, something more is needed in order to set about the work of composition itself, and that is an often very painful effort to place ourselves directly at the heart of the subject, and to seek, as deeply as possible, an impulse, after which we need only let ourselves go.

Hence it follows that the highest art will always be the most individual, the most unique. As he says in *Laughter:*

What the artist fixes on his canvas is something he has seen at a certain spot, on a certain day, at a certain hour, with a colouring that will never be seen again. What the poet sings of is a certain mood which was his, and his alone, and which will never return . . . We may indeed, give general names to these feelings, but they cannot be the same thing in another soul. They are individualised. Thereby, and thereby only, do they belong to art; for generalities, symbols, or even types form the current coin of our daily perception. How then does misunderstanding on this point arise?

Proust writes in a similar vein in *The Past Recaptured.*

Only the subjective impression, however inferior the material may seem to be and however improbable the outline, is a criterion of truth and for that reason it alone merits being apprehended by the mind, for it alone is able, if the mind can extract this truth, to lead the mind to a greater perfection and impart to it a pure joy. The subjective impression is for the writer what experimentation is for the scientist, but with this difference, that with the scientist the work of the intelligence precedes, and with the writer it comes afterwards. Anything we have not had to decipher and clarify by our own personal effort, anything that was clear before we intervened, is not our own. And since art is a faithful recomposing of life, around these truths that one had attained within oneself there floats an atmosphere of poetry, the sweetness of a mystery, which is merely the semi-darkness through which we have come.

Bergson had the same conception of nature, which he shared with Baudelaire and the Symbolists, and that was that nature had no beauty in herself, that she had no colour or line. Nature was beautiful only by what the artist brought to her of himself. In *Time and Free-Will*, Bergson says: "We might ask ourselves whether Nature is beautiful otherwise than through the meeting by chance of certain processes of art, and whether art is not prior to nature." Proust says:

Thus I had already come to the conclusion that we are not at all free in the presence of the work of art to be created, that we do not do it as we ourselves please, but that it existed prior to us, and we should seek to discover it as we would do a natural law because it is both necessary and hidden. But when art enabled us to make this discovery, was it not disclosing to us, after all, what we ought to hold most precious but what usually remains forever unknown to us, our true life, reality as we have felt it, so different from what we think that we are filled with great happiness when chance brings back to us the true remembrance of it? I convinced myself of this by the falseness of even the art that calls itself "realist," which would not be so untruthful if we had not formed in life the habit of giving to our sensations an outward expression so different from them, which, after a short while, we take for reality itself.

Bergson led the writers of his age into the regions to which they naturally aspired, where they could breathe freely, where they began to realize that there exists a spiritual reality. Most of Proust's work is an exposition of Bergson's philosophy. Proust also forced his readers to accept the inexpressible. His theory of memory resembles that of Bergson, in seeing the difference between habit memory and pure memory—the first is physiological and the second psychological and spiritual. Bergson says in *Matter and Memory:*

Memory, distinct from the material, protects and preserves the real part of the past, and puts it out of the way of the utilitarian dispersion of the present. When it liberates it, as sleep liberates the images of the dream, it is transfigured. It has the whole of its value, it is integrated into eternity.

Bergson's doctrine may not have altered the course of philosophical reflection, but he did affect literary thought, and what writers call philosophy, with the result that the focus of personality was no longer intelligence, but intuition and feeling; and that the most precious intimation of experience, the immediate data of consciousness, was considered, at best, half conscious, and capable only of being revealed to the artist's probing.

Bergson's views of the problems which confront modern civilization are as true today as when he expressed them thirty years ago. He understood how, without further spiritual development, the world could not continue to live. The words which end his last work, published in 1932, *Morality and Religion,* are tragically apposite for the sixth decade of the twentieth century, in an atomic age. Those who today read Baudelaire in search for a remedy to our ills, in a desire to find something new which will lift mankind out of its rut, will find similar spiritual food in Bergson:

But whether we go bail for small measures or great, a decision is imperative. Mankind lies groaning, half-crushed beneath the weight of its own progress. Men do not sufficiently realise that their future is in their own hands. Theirs is the task of determining first of all whether they want to go on living or not. Theirs the responsibility, then, for deciding if they want merely to live, or intend to make just the extra effort required for fulfilling, even on their refractory planet, the essential function of the universe, which is a machine for the making of gods.

PART TWO

The Bergson Centennial
at Paris

by Jean Hyppolite

(AT THE ÉCOLE NORMALE SUPÉRIEURE)

A tribute to Bergson should not ignore the formative years of the philosopher, which may have been decisive in the orientation of his thought. Bergson had at first dreamed of becoming a mathematician. Instead of staying in the philosophy class a second year and preparing for *Normale-Lettres*, he began elementary mathematics; he took a *concours général* prize in mathematics in 1876 and proposed an elegant solution to a geometrical question found in a letter from Pascal to Fermat. But in spite of his remarkable gifts Bergson preferred to return to philosophy and prepared for *Normales-Lettres*, where he took third place in 1878. Such a dual vocation is not unusual here, where science and literature coexist, where even in this very year a first-ranking science candidate has turned to philosophy and a philosophy student to mathematical research.

The leading candidate of 1878 was Jaurès. We have some memories of the youthful relationship between Jaurès and Bergson, whose careers were to differ so greatly. From the first there was a great contrast between the two, between

the expansive eloquence of one and the subtlety, the medi-
tative spirit, of the other. They went together to the Louvre.
Their schoolmates sometimes amused themselves by setting
them against one another. There is a story that one of their
professors, Desjardins, proposed that they reenact Cicero's
oration defending Fonteius against a charge of lying. Jaurès attacked vigorously: "Fonteius could have been ac-
quitted in an era when the republic was declining, but you
who judge him at the beginning of the republic will con-
demn him." Their classmates were at first carried away
by Jaurès' eloquence, but Bergson was able to persuade
them with elegance, distinction, and a splendidly solid
argument. The result of this debate—which we can scarcely
imagine today—was a draw. The classmates who were to
give the decision could award victory neither to Jaurès nor
to Bergson. They uttered neither "absolvo" nor "con-
demno" but "non liquet." We also know that Bergson took
fencing lessons and that his teacher one day told him, "You
are subtle, Mr. Bergson."

I have not time to recreate the three years Bergson passed
at the École—the first year was devoted to obtaining the
licentiate, the second to acquiring a diploma known at that
time as a *définitif*, the third, at last, to the *agrégation*. The
question was: would Jaurès or Bergson take first place in
the *agrégation?* Jaurès possibly antagonized the examiners
by the large audience which came to hear him and by his
excessive eloquence. Lesbazeilles, who appeared alone before the examiners, took first place, Bergson second, and
Jaurès third.

At this time students of the École enjoyed less freedom than today; they might go out only on Thursdays and Sundays. We may imagine long conversations among the students, in the monastic corridors of the École, or in the courtyard, around the fish pond. Lucien Lévy-Bruhl was a third-year student when Bergson was an undergraduate; he who became Monseigneur Baudrillard was, as well as Jaurès, a fellow student of Bergson's. Perhaps the most interesting thing about this house is the diversity of minds which meet here and the mutual education that is a result. There has always been a love of freedom, discussion, and even paradox. Bergson was a student librarian, and therefore had free access to the library, where he studied Spencer and read Lachelier. His masters were Durkheim, Ollé-Laprune, Boutroux. We know that he then sought his way more in the philosophy of Spencer than in the Kantian critique.

Before his professorship at the Collège de France Bergson returned to the École Normale as a lecturer. In 1898 (shortly after the publication of *Matter and Memory*) he gave at the École some notable lectures on ancient philosophy. He did not always have a large audience, because he was accused of not preparing his students specifically for the *agrégation*. When he was Professor for Advanced Students at the Henry IV School, he had as a student Thibaudet, who, it seems to me, has written one of the best and most suggestive books on him. At the École he met Charles Péguy, author of *Jeanne d'Arc*, who was to give Bergsonism its great existential dimensions.

The year 1911–12 to which I refer was evidently a peak (I do not say the peak, but a peak) in Bergson's career. It was the time, for one thing, when he had just given the lectures at Oxford on "The Perception of Change" and, for another thing, had presented, at the Bologna convention, the famous paper on "Philosophical Intuition." I shall surprise no one by saying that something of all that found its way into the classrooms of the Lycée Louis-le-Grand, although no one among us had the audacity to think that he could "cut" his classes on Friday or Saturday and slip into Bergson's courses. Many reasons prevented us. I must state that our professor of philosophy that year had never been counted among the Bergsonians. This was Marcel Bernès. He had before him students who had been initiated into philosophy by Bergsonian professors; such was my case. I had had at Dijon a strongly convinced one, Albert Sauvage; my good friend François Saleilles had had at Stanislas a teacher who since has taught in this house, Jean Baruzi. He was a fervent Bergsonian. Certainly Bernès tried neither to "Bergsonize" nor to "de-Bergsonize" us, but it was apparent that some of Bergson's preoccupations and something of his way of approaching problems were present in his teaching. I never suspected this more strongly than recently, when I went over the yearbooks of the Collège de France for that period to see what Bergson had said in the course of the years preceding 1911. I remembered then the way in which Bernès always spoke of "the posing of the question," how he taught us that it was more important to pose questions than to produce some acceptable solution. And I can better explain to myself, too, why he gave us a whole year's course on Berkeley. For two years Bergson had studied, in that classroom, the writings of Berkeley, and when Bernès came to the end of his course he offered us as dessert, so to speak, the paper of the Bologna Convention. I can still hear the inflection with which he toned down the irony of the passage on the hodgepodge one can make with pieces, conveniently adapted, of what the historians of philosophy are able to find in Berkeley's work.

And then I should recall a memory which, for, me, is rather moving; on a fine April Sunday in that year I was taken to the hall of the Société de Geographie by another friend of mine, Élie Gounelle, who was the son of a Protestant minister. He was involved with the organization "Foi et Vie" which arranged lectures, and therefore I had the greatly envied privilege of hearing Bergson's lecture, "Soul and Body." We were, Gounelle and I, readers, very attentive young readers, of *Matter and Memory;* we were surprised to find the fundamental themes of the book approached in a new way. I shall speak not of Bergson's voice, of the very great charm which emanated from that voice, but of the perfection with which everything was set forth and the value given to images. There I heard comparisons now famous, concerning the relationship of brain and thought: that of the peg from which a garment hangs, which will fall if this support falls, although there is no analogous relationship between one and the other; also the image of the orchestra leader's baton. Many things in that lecture must have struck young listeners. The man's complete lack of complacency about what he was saying; his severity and austerity, in spite of the brilliant style, took a strong hold on us.

Allow me, in ending this detour into my youthful memories, to recall the impression of great soberness with which Bergson struck me when I had a chance to observe him several years later. It was at the time of a mission to Spain, in 1916—he undertook, with several of his Institute colleagues, a good-will tour for France, then at war. I had the opportunity, since I was not yet conscripted, of living in Seville on a scholarship, and I was able to be of some service to the academicians, who took me with them to Granada. Two pictures of Bergson in Spain remain with me. One evening in Seville, seated near him at dinner, I saw him, while joining in the conversation as far as courtesy required, abstain from that collective devouring of a certain number of dishes that is called a banquet; his dinner was a bun and a glass of milk. A picture of sobriety, fortuitous perhaps, but one that struck me. Another picture, the authenticity of which I can vouch for, is that of Bergson silently admiring, by moonlight, the Court of the Myrtles at Granada. Someone had been kind enough to take us to see the Alhambra at night, after having shown it to us by day. This silent Bergson, his eyes opened wide to the nocturnal scene, has remained for me a symbol of the restraint and the capacity for silence in a man so eloquent in his fashion. He opposed to *homo sapiens* and *homo faber*, *homo loquax*, which seemed to him to contrast as awkwardly with one as with the other. He was, he who spoke so well, exactly the opposite of *homo loquax.*

Now let us turn again to the subject of his teaching. That lecture on the soul and the body, which gave me a direct experience of an incomparable art of persuasion—on this subject I now ask myself a question which I did not ask then, but which is incumbent on one whose duty it is to chronicle Bergson's teaching at the Collège de France, even though he did not take any of his courses. Was what I heard in the hall of the Société de Géographie like a lecture in one of Bergson's courses? I reply with considerable assurance: No, after having talked to some of his students. We heard there, evidently, a synthesis of many lectures. In a note to *La Pensée et le Mouvant* Bergson, discussing his views on what he calls "the choreography of discourse" (another way of expressing the relationship of thought and bodily activity), tells us that he has there condensed a lecture given at the Collège de France on the rhythm of philosophical discourse. He tells how, reading aloud certain passages of Descartes, he had shown that rhythm was essential to the communication of the thought expressed in those passages. Well, it is certain that if in this page Bergson summed up a whole lecture given within these walls, the lecture entitled "Soul and Body" condensed many others, within a new form. All I have heard on the subject of Bergson's courses has convinced me that he felt the course to be a unity, that from beginning to end he closely related each lesson to the preceding one, repeating

at the beginning of each one the essential point he felt he
had established in the preceding lecture. It was a technique
wholly different from the one he used in the "Foi et Vie"
lecture. This leads us to ask what connection Bergson's
courses had with the written expression of his thought: the
books he has left us.

I think the question is not without value, if only to put
us on guard against a commonplace that we hear often
enough: for a professor of the Collège de France, to give
a course is to prepare a book; the book will be molded by
the outlines of the course. It is true in a certain number of
cases, but not so often as people think, and for Bergson it
was rarely the case. I should simply note that when Bergson came to the Collège de France he had already published
not only *Time and Free Will* but also *Matter and Memory*,
and if we look for a connection between his teaching here
(as far as we can tell what it was by the résumés in our
yearbooks) and the books which followed, we are struck
by the fact that the only subject revealing a close connection is that of the course of 1904–1905, on the evolution
of the problem of freedom, a course which shows an obvious relationship, by its subject, with *Creative Evolution,*
which was to appear soon thereafter.

A summary of the courses taught at the Collège de
France in the following years, in the chair of Modern Philosophy (I shall refer later to this title) offers us, in turn,
will, effort, general ideas and the posing of problems—we
find again "the posing of the question"!—the nature of
wit, personality. A course which came just after the Oxford

lectures entailed a probing of the idea of evolution and the proposal of a sort of program for reforming the understanding. Then there was "Spirituality and Freedom." "Philosophic Method" was the last course taught by Bergson at the Collège de France, in 1913–14. I must point out that in all the lectures given by Bergson between 1900 and 1914 one sees nothing that leads, however indirectly, to *The Two Sources of Morality and Religion*, the book of his old age. It would not seem a betrayal of the spirit of the oral teaching he did, here to say that he devoted himself above all to going more deeply into the problems he had already broached in *Matter and Memory*, if not even earlier in *Time and Free Will*, or, later, in *Creative Evolution*.

He was very demanding of himself in the written expression of that which he wanted to set down as a more or less definitive statement of his thought. He forbade anyone to take possession of provisional statements, which might have been obtained during a lecture. I think we should consider that the years at the Collège de France were for him and his disciples—for he had disciples—extremely fecund because of the way in which he explored problems, and the way in which he applied to new questions views he had already presented. It seems to me that this is what the Collège meant to Bergson: the possibility of communicating, of setting forth orally what he had already basically formulated in several main books.

I apologize for not giving the Collège de France a handsomer role—I would be afraid of falsifying the real significance of Bergson's oral exposition; in returning it to

its true value we are not underrating it. I think that Bergson's accomplishment in this lecture room, by word, was
immense.

It is necessary now, since the role of chronicler has fallen
to me, to give you some indications of what Bergson's professorial career at the Collège de France was, details that
you already are not ill acquainted with and that others
could easily learn, as I myself have done, by spending a
few hours with the archives of the Collège de France and
its collection of yearbooks.

I have said that Bergson lectured in the chair of "Modern
Philosophy." He did not begin there, and this is the role
played by accident in some professorial careers. In 1897–
98 he substituted for Charles Lévêque, professor of Greek
and Latin philosophy. When the death of Nourisson left
the chair of Modern Philosophy vacant, most of the professors of the Collège de France thought that Bergson
would become its occupant. The report which Ribot presented to the Assembly expressed at length the importance
he attributed to Bergson: he defined him as "a metaphysician, but one who links all his speculations to positive
research," emphasizing that this mind "both subtle and dynamic" already counted "many enthusiastic disciples
among the young." This was in 1899. Three days before
the Collège made its recommendation for filling the chair
that it had earmarked for Bergson, Lévêque died in his
turn. Those who had supported the cause of Gabriel de
Tarde against the candidacy of Bergson had the opportu-

nity to say: "Bergson will have his turn; Tarde can only hold the chair of Modern Philosophy, so let us reserve Bergson for the one in Greek and Latin philosophy." And this is how Gabriel de Tarde was named, in fact, professor of Modern Philosophy, and Bergson, for several years, taught Ancient Philosophy. In the autumn of 1904 the death of Tarde allowed Bergson, thanks to a procedure rare in the Collège but one which we followed not long ago for the chair of Medicine, to be transferred to the chair which suited him best. The Assembly made the proposal and the Ministry soon ratified his nomination as professor of Modern Philosophy.

Bergson had enthusiastic disciples; he had ardent hearers, and I cannot refrain from mentioning, at least in passing, a picturesque aspect of his success in his courses. Those who know nothing else about Bergson's lectures at the Collège de France know this, at least. The lecture room was invaded well ahead of time. This audience, it is often said, was composed of society people, people having no profound interest in philosophy. But who can judge? The matter reached a critical point in 1914, at the beginning of the year; it was probably the election of Bergson to the Académie Française that precipitated this phenomenon, the rush to his philosophy course. Progressively the room became more inadequate. Means of transmitting sound from one room to another had not yet been invented; in short, a solution had to be found to reserve a certain number of places for students in the classroom; it was divided so as to reserve a part of it for them. You will see, at the exposition which we will soon visit,[1] a petition to this effect, signed by many young people, some of whom have since become more or less well known. The Administrator then received violent protests against this measure which, in effect, excluded some of the public from the room. Bergson must have been troubled, for certainly the tradition of the Collège de France, if not its rule, has been that its courses should be public, open to every mind which claims, or hopes, to enrich itself by attending them. It was perhaps a little rash to say that Bergson attracted "society people." We must agree that this spiritual revolution spoken of by Étienne Gilson—the restoration of metaphysics to the first generations of the twentieth century—took many paths, and that not all of these were the paths of professional philosophers. We understand, then, that Bergson must have been perturbed by a success which, as we say today, "dazzled" the public, but in unfortunate circumstances which excluded part of the audience that wished to hear him.

During his career in the chair of Modern Philosophy Bergson twice had a substitute. There was at that time an arrangement, which remains in present-day regulations, but has fallen into disuse, which permitted a professor to furnish his replacement; the substitute he chose was then proposed to the minister by the Assembly, a procedure which excluded arbitrary designations. The professor received half of the year's salary and the substitute the other

[1] Bergson exposition organized at the Bibliothèque Nationale.

half. This custom justified itself for many years, notably in that there were almost no retirements at the Collège de France: Bergson's first substitute was Couturat, in 1905–6, the year when he was preparing *Creative Evolution* for publication. In 1909–10 he had as substitute René Worms. Finally, his permanent substitute from 1914 until 1920–21 was Édouard Le Roy, who was to become his successor. The regulation provided that substitution for a professor should not continue for more than five consecutive years, and the immense respect that Bergson inspired in his colleagues slightly extended the limit in his favor. But he himself had too much respect for the house in which he taught to agree to this stretching of the regulations, and he asked to be retired in 1921. We find in certain works (certain dictionaries) totally erroneous information on this matter. Bergson stopped teaching at the Collège de France early, when he was sixty-one years old. Many others, at this period, taught until they were seventy-five and even older. I think this retirement must be explained by the high conception that Bergson had of teaching. He considered that his lectures demanded a great deal of meditation and a serious attempt at perfection. During the years when he taught at the Collège de France he held himself most scrupulously to the common rule of a minimum number of required courses, but it is understandable enough that at a certain point in his career he wanted to be freed of this burden which weighed upon him. It is one more reason for us to respect his memory in this house. Bergson set for himself a very high conception of teaching

by *Gaston Berger*

(AT THE SORBONNE)

Mr. Gouhier, in a very fine paper he has just presented to the Académie des Science Morales et Politiques, has said that the philosophy of Bergson was a philosophy of nature. If it is so—and for my part I think that it is—a reflection on Bergsonian thought and a critique of Bergson's themes and theses ought not to consist in judging this philosophy from points of view alien to it, or comparing it with the statements made by philosophers who have other preoccupations. If Bergson describes nature, then isn't the best procedure that of going to the things themselves to see what they look like, and to compare the portrait with the model which has inspired it? If this procedure is the suitable one here, perhaps we should take note that Bergson's contemporaries were not well placed to use it. Without doubt, to understand a philosophy we must place it in its own epoch: thus we may better lay hold on the connections of the thought, because we know what theses the philosopher is opposing and what difficulties he is trying to overcome. However, this retrospective method is not, perhaps

the one which should be applied to a philosophy of creation, and of novelty. If we think of the world of 1880,
of 1900, of 1910, to which Bergson addressed himself, we
see it marked by weariness and lassitude. It does not correspond merely to the end of a century. It marks the end
of an epoch. The great enthusiasm which created the Renaissance has cooled off; the heavy tedium which crushes
Baudelaire weighs on everyone's shoulders. Doubtless,
people speak of evolution, but a cooled-off evolution, an
evolution of the past, an evolution which may once have
created things but for a long time has created nothing and
contents itself with developing, then progressively water-
ing down its earlier creations. Man himself, who seems to
mark the end of this evolution, moves no further and can
no longer change. Doubtless people speak a great deal of
progress, but by this word they understand a sort of automatic transformation, in short, mechanism. The biologists,
on their side, apply themselves to rediscovering the mechanism of evolution, not its creative surge.

On the contrary, the men of today, who live in this com-
plicated, changeable, surprising, disturbing world which
is ours, are in a better position than Bergson's contemporaries to understand his message. Two years ago certain
men met to share their knowledge, especially their personal experiences, and to reflect together on the problem of
the future. The fruit of their meditations was a description
of the world, particularly the human world, which was that
of a Bergsonian universe. A philosophy of mobility yesterday could surprise and disappoint those who placed their

hopes in the static and who sought to explain movement
from the static. Today a philosophy of mobility expresses
only the most evident and constant of experiences. We are
well aware today that everything changes, that everything
changes rapidly, that everything changes more and more
rapidly; we are well aware that each new discovery at once
raises up ten others; we are well aware that each difficulty
solved gives birth to ten new difficulties, no less serious than
the one over which we have just triumphed, but which generally oblige us to modify our attitude and invent new
methods of solution. The surging forth of which Bergson
speaks in his books is no longer just a metaphor for us: it
is the direct translation of an immediate experience. We
know that the rigid and inert products of this surge fall
back and the creative *élan* ceaselessly makes its way
through this matter, these mechanisms, these habits which
constantly threaten to crush us. Now this, too, has become
a daily experience for us: as there are too many cars in
our streets, there is too much specialized knowledge in our
curricula, there are too many books in our libraries, too
many documents in our card indexes, too many rules made
to support us, which only serve to paralyze us. It is through
this whole mass of increasingly heavy and dense creations
of yesterday, thoroughly cooled off, that we must trace
our way. Man is threatened by his works; he is first of all
encumbered by his works. The surge which creates things
and the decline of things which disintegrate are no longer
arbitrary images for us, but are the very description of
what we see. What the simplest reflection shows us is the

unforeseeability of the future. We meet here an ambivalence, an ambiguity, which is not a weakness of Bergsonism, but which was, quite rightly, denounced by Bergson.
The future is unforeseeable, and if we believe that ma-
chines will think for us and automatically predict for us
the shape that the world will take tomorrow, we shall be
seriously deceived. But meanwhile, in evoking this unforeseeable future, we are well aware that we cannot rely on
a sort of easygoing intuition. One is often tempted to confuse intuition with a free gift or with a more or less vague
presentiment. Now here is the paradox: this unforeseeable
future—we have to apply ourselves to forecasting certain
aspects of it with all the care, all the attention, and all the
strictness possible, while knowing only that our forecasts,
while indispensable, will remain insufficient. It is the same
as with the concepts which it has sometimes been said
Bergson wished to do without, but which, on the contrary,
he claimed to have a certain value if we do not ask more of
them than they can give. We must use forecasts, like ma-
chines, to construct human happiness. Necessary and insufficient: the two things are linked; this is perhaps one of
Bergson's greatest discoveries. Intuition never dispenses
with work. The concept is at once what hinders us if we
take it as an absolute, and what aids us if we are able to
find in it a means.

The philosophy of surging forth also has an amazing,
even paradoxical consequence: it is that life does not age;
that creation, in its activity, far from exhausting itself, becomes richer and stronger. Its *élan* never stops increasing.

Bodies age; the *élan vital* seems to rejuvenate itself. The philosophy of Bergson, which must be judged as a description, not as a system, is for modern man a faithful description. It does not place itself, however, as one might think, in opposition to traditional metaphysics. I remember that one day, referring to the terms of one of our conversations, I wrote to Bergson to point out that there must be a profound difference between the mystique of Life and the mystique of Being. Bergson replied that this difference undoubtedly existed, but that it tended to diminish to the extent that we were able to increase our mastery of Nature. Thus, also, the conquest of the spiritual life itself, access to plenitude, the discovery of profound joy—all of this supposes, implies, demands work. The philosophy of Bergson, far from saying that everything goes well and goes of itself, far from putting us to sleep with a melody that lulls us with illusions, is a call to laborious creation. Thus, while restoring men to the great philosophical view which permits them to attain joy and which gives hope back to them, it recalls the place which men must give to suffering and work. The mystique is no longer the scorn of technique, but its utilization.

by Gabriel Marcel

(AT THE SORBONNE)

Bergson—I pronounce this name; I hold it in myself; I strive to awaken from a long sleep the magic powers which formerly, half a century ago, this name released around itself. As always in such circumstances, I note that what is so distant is at the same time quite close, immediate, present. I see him again at the Collège de France, entering the amphitheater where we submitted to the course of Mr. Leroi-Beaulieu—submitted, rather than listened—so as to be there when he arrived. And again I sense the charm which he exercised on us all. Nothing could be further from the spell produced by certain orators. Bergson was no orator, thank God, for an orator creates around him a zone of passivity, in which the hearers gather as though to merge with each other by a strange and, on the whole, disquieting phenomenon of agglutination. Listening to Bergson, on the contrary, everyone felt himself more closely attached to himself and at the same time fulfilled, even to overflowing—fulfilled [*exaucé*] and at the same moment uplifted [*exhaussé*]. This sort of half-pun, with which I

have often tried to express the melody crowning a poem,
I am tempted to repeat to express the feeling of inner expansion that Bergson awoke in all of us. I speak here of
Bergson the professor, not of the man I visited first in the
Rue Vital and later in the Boulevard Beauséjour. The emotion which these visits aroused in me was not of the same
order. At the Collège de France it seemed to me that I was
never present at one of his classes without being stirred by
the hope that a revelation would be given me, without the
assurance that I would welcome it, that we were, if I may
say so, side by side; my eagerness was so great that I re-
belled a little when at the beginning of the class I heard
him repeat patiently, meticulously—and, for me, unavail-
ingly—what he had told us a week earlier with perfect
clarity; it seemed to me that these minutes were like im-
proper deductions from the time of the revelation. We can
never regret sufficiently that at that time there were no
phonograph records or tapes to preserve the unique quality
of his speech. When I grope for a word with which to express it, the first one that occurs to me is the doubtless unusual one "felicity." With Frédéric Rauh, for example,
or even with Léon Brunschvicg, the speech was, if not weak,
at least a little stumbling; with Victor Delbos it had something almost too deliberate or magisterial; with Bergson it
was permeated by the pleasant tremor that vibrates in the
voice of an explorer when he tries to evoke the ineffable
peace of some inviolate shore or perhaps a sojourn in the
midst of a fabulous tribe. The words of charm and magic
correspond, it seems to me, in some manner to this experi-

the language of Nietzsche mightn't we be tempted to place the philosopher of the *élan vital* among the Dionysian spirits? But we could not do so, I think, except by virtue of a misunderstanding that must be avoided. Like the Ariane of Maeterlinck and of Dukas, Bergson had the passion of clarity. It would not be absurd, despite appearances, to say that for him life remains in a certain way—this would demand careful shading of meaning—in a certain way, idea. What is extremely novel in Bergson is the tender precaution he takes in approaching his subject, as though he were delicately brushing aside vines to bend over a sleeping infant. The more I absorb myself in the evocation of those hours at the Collège de France, the more I assure myself that they were in truth traversed by the current of an unrestrainable hope. I use this word more readily than "optimism." On the metaphysical plane all optimism seems to lead either to Leibnitz or to the *Minores*, whose names have hardly survived into the present time, but the spirit of Leibnitz did not preside over Bergson's courses. Leaving out of account, be it understood, Taine, Spencer, and some contemporaries, his references, explicit or not, were neo-Platonic or Berkeleian. I am thinking here, of course, of the Berkeley of *Siris*, not that of the *Dialogues*. This may seem strange today. How could a philosophy of pure duration claim kinship with Plotinus? And yet, nevertheless, it was so. Bergson pronounced the name of Plotinus with a sort of shy dilection. And I note moreover, in passing, that if my lamented colleague, the noble and profound historian Émile Bréhier, was able to give his adherence to Bergson's thought, this may have been because of his Alexandrian attachments. At any rate, we may be certain that the future historians of philosophy will place Henri Bergson in a metaphysical context infinitely more vast than could have been believed by those of his contemporaries who were content to place him in relation to such and such a philosopher of the nineteenth century or the beginning of the twentieth. I am thinking especially of one of his detractors whose pamphlets had their hour of fame and who so strangely failed to recognize the essential rhythm of a doctrine of which we must say that, by ways hitherto untrodden, despite all, it rejoins at the peak certain intuitions of the *Philosophia perennis*.

What nonetheless surprised us—us who heard him in 1908 and 1909—was the confidence of the tone with which he spoke of those who would come after him, those who would toil in their turn to build the new science for which he thought he had laid the first stones. One question comes to our mind, when we reflect on his assurance, which, I affirm, was far from all presumptuousness. The intuition, singular and creative, without which he did not conceive philosophy, or at least metaphysics, to be worthy of the name, this intuition which was the root of his work, what sort of relationship could it have with the new science or with the scientific metaphysics of which he thought himself only one of the first fashioners? It is not very easy to answer this question. I am inclined to believe that in his eyes the nature of this science was able to display itself only by

such intuitions as could, alone, give access to life considered genuinely creative in its growth. Perhaps, not
without reason, if we were to ask such a question, it would
invite us to distinguish between science as it is, as it consti-
tutes itself in its own dynamism, and the accounts *a pos-
teriori* to which it can and must inevitably give place
among those entrusted with teaching it. But they, to tell the
truth, too often run the risk of falsifying its progress and
of proposing a schematic representation that we have to
shatter or—at least—to overcome to think of it in its in-
ventive movement. Perhaps, moreover—it is a hypothesis
which I would gladly enough adopt—it would be advisable
to admit in what we wrongly call Bergsonism a certain irreducible dualism, and here there is a Blondelian distinction between *la pensée pensante* and *la pensée pensée* that
I insist on appealing to, asking myself, moreover, if one
would not touch upon, by this obliquity, the late, but so
fruitful distinction between the closed and the open.

What must be recognized, nonetheless, is that the hope
of Bergson has been—until now, at least—in a large measure frustrated. He had, certainly, in every country, many
disciples. But can we say that these disciples were his
successors in the sense he expected? It seems to me not,
and I shall add that we are all little inclined to compare
him to an artisan, placing the first stones of a cathedral or
of a pyramid. I would be tempted to ask myself here
whether Henri Bergson was not often deluded as to himself, and the true nature of his contribution, by his care
not only to maintain the closest contact with positive sci-

winian type? But such tensions, far from weakening the range of the works in the midst of which we find them, contribute towards making them more richly educational for us, to the same degree that such works already transcend themselves. In this perspective I will say that the greatness of Bergson in my eyes consists much less in what one might otherwise unwisely call his system than in the fact that he was and is a *fountainhead*. Two of the greatest works of our time, without a doubt, could not have existed without him: that of Péguy, on one hand, that of Proust, on the other. But the prodigious gap between these two careers reveals in a certain paradoxical fashion the unequaled driving power which was the endowment of the brilliant inspirer to whom we are paying homage.

I should like to close with a brief remark. Paradoxically enough, it was the fashion, in certain philosophical circles, not long ago, in circles where *engagement* was preached, to hold up to ridicule what was called "l'esprit de sérieux." I fear there has been some confusion here. Whatever it may be, if, as I think, the true spirit of the serious is an attention to reality, that is not only demanding but incorruptible, Bergson has given us one of the highest examples of it in the history of thought. This I say particularly for the sake of the young philosophers who in their turn will set forth on the paths of speculative adventure. May they, beyond all divergences, all possible objections, not only greet with gratitude and humility this conspicuous virtue, but find it an incentive to their own quest. For if, never been a Bergsonian school—his reputation was enormous. It was not until more recent times that there appeared a shadowy post-Bergsonism, exclusive, as if one did not better honor Bergson by admitting that he belongs to everybody.

How could the one who had radically transformed philosophy and literature become this almost canonical author? Had he changed? We shall see that he changed little. Or had he changed his public, winning it over to his own audacity? The truth is that there are two Bergsonisms: that of audacity, when the philosophy of Bergson fought and, says Péguy, fought well; and that which came after the victory, persuaded in advance of what Bergson had spent a long time in finding, already supplied with concepts which Bergson had made for himself. Identified with the vague cause of spiritualism, or of some other entity, the Bergsonian intuitions lose their bite; they are generalized, minimized. This is only a retrospective or exterior Bergsonism. It found its formula when Father Sertillanges wrote that the Church today no longer placed Bergson on the Index, not because it revoked its judgment of 1914, but because it now knew the final direction of his works. Bergson himself did not wait to find out where his road led before he took it or, rather, made it. He did not wait for the *Two Sources* before permitting himself *Matter and Memory* or *Creative Evolution*. Yet if the *Two Sources* compensated for the condemned works, it would not have had its meaning without them, it would not have been so famous without them. Take it or leave it, we cannot have

truth without danger. It isn't philosophy if one thinks first
of the conclusions. The philosopher does not look for short
cuts; he goes the whole route, and a definitive Bergsonism
distorts Bergson. Bergson disturbed; it reassures. Bergson
was a conquest; Bergsonism defends, justifies Bergson.
Bergson was a contact with things; Bergsonism is a collection of accepted opinions. The conciliations, the celebrations should not make us forget the pathway that Bergson
traced alone and that he never renounced: this direct, so-
ber, immediate, and unusual manner of remaking philosophy, of seeking the profound in the apparent and the absolute under our very eyes—in short, in its most proper
sense, the spirit of discovery which is the fountainhead of
Bergsonism.

He ended his course in 1911 by these words, which the
review *Les Études* preserved: "If the researcher, the artist,
the philosopher attach themselves to the pursuit of fame,
it is because they lack the absolute security of having
created something capable of living. Give them this assurance, and you will at once see them make light of the fuss
that is made over them." The only thing that he wanted in
the end was to have written books that would live. Now as
to that testimony, we can give it only by indicating how
present he is in our labors, how in some pages of his work,
we, with our preferences and our partialities, feel, as did
his hearers of 1900, that he is at the heart of the matter.

He is a philosopher first of all by the manner in which
he discovered the whole of philosophy, as if for the first

time, through the examination of one of the mechanical principles which Spencer used without strictness. It is thus that he perceived that we do not approach time by grasping it, as though between pincers, between measuring lines, but that it is necessary, on the contrary, if we are to conceive it, to let it act freely, to go along with the continual birth which makes it always new and, because always new, always the same.

His philosopher's view found something else, more than he had sought. For if that is time, it is not something that I see from the outside. From the outside I would have only an outline of it, I would not be in the face of the generating thrust. Time, then, is myself; I am the duration that I grasp; the duration that grasps itself is in me. And already we are in the absolute. Strange absolute knowledge, since we know neither all our memories nor even the whole density of our present; and my contact with myself is "partial coincidence"—a word which Bergson often used and which, indeed, poses a problem. At all events, when it is a question of myself, it is because the contact is partial that it is absolute, it is because I am engaged in my duration that I know it as an individual, it is because it inundates me that I have an experience of it which could not be conceived of as being any closer or more intimate. Absolute knowledge is not an observation flight, it is inherency. This is a great novelty in 1889, and for the future, gives as a principle to philosophy, not an I think and its immanent thoughts, but a Being-itself, the cohesion of which is also an uprooting.

Since it is here that I coincide with a noncoincidence, the experience is capable of being extended beyond the particular being that I am. The intuition of my duration is an apprenticeship in a general manner of seeing, the principle of a sort of Bergsonian "reduction" which reconsiders all things *sub specie durationis*—what we call subject, what we call object, and even what we call space: for we already see taking form a space within, an extension, which is the world where Achilles walks. There are beings, structures, like a melodic line (Bergson says: "organizations"), which are only a certain way of enduring. Duration is not only change, growth, mobility, it is being—in the living and active sense of the word. Time has not taken the place of being; it is understood as nascent being, and it is now the entire being that must be approached from the side of time.

This was apparent when *Matter and Memory* appeared, or at least it should have been apparent. But the book evoked surprise; it appeared obscure; it is, even today, the least read of Bergson's great books. Nevertheless, it is here that the scope of duration and the method of intuition are expanded in a decisive manner. Forgetting, as he said, his previous book, following for its own sake another line of facts, making contact with the compound of soul and body, Bergson was led back to duration. But duration took on in that different approach new dimensions, and we would be ignoring the law of a philosophy that claims to be not a system but a full reflection and that wishes to make being speak, if we here reproach Bergson with the charge of a veering of direction, when this is the quest itself. Henceforth, duration is the medium in which soul and body are connected, because the present and the body, the past and the spirit, different in nature, nevertheless pass into each other. Intuition is decidedly no more simple coincidence than fusion: it extends itself to "limits," like pure perception and pure memory, and also to their interstice, to a being that, Bergson says, opens itself to the present and to space in the exact measure that it aims at a future and disposes of a past. There is a life—Maurice Blondel would say a "hybridization"—of the intuitions, a "dual release" towards matter and towards memory. It is by taking the opposites in their great difference that intuition sees them rejoin.

For example, it would greatly distort Bergson to minimize the amazing description of perceived being given in *Matter and Memory*. He does not at all say that things are, in the restrictive sense, images, mental or otherwise,—he says that their fullness under my regard is such that it is as if my vision took place in them rather than in myself, as if to be seen were only a degradation of their eminent being, as if being "represented"—to appear, Bergson says, in the "camera obscura" of the subject—far from being their definition, resulted from their natural profuseness! Never before had anyone established this circuit between being and myself, which has the result that being is "for me," the spectator, but that in return the spectator is "for being." Never before had anyone thus described the brute being of the perceived world. In unveiling it along

with nascent duration, Bergson rediscovers in the heart of
man a pre-Socratic and "prehuman" sense of the world.

Duration and Simultaneity, which is, Bergson repeats, a
book of philosophy, is placed yet more firmly in the perceived world. Today, as thirty-five years ago, physicists
reproach Bergson for introducing the observer into rela-
tivistic physics, which, they say, can make time relative
only with instruments of measurement or a system of reference. But what Bergson wishes to show is precisely that
there is no simultaneity between things in themselves,
which, no matter how contiguous they may be, remain individuals. Only perceived things can participate in the
same line of the present—and, in return, as soon as there
is perception there is immediately, and with no other measurement, simultaneity of a single view, not only between
two events in the same field but even between all perceptive
fields, all observers, all durations. If one took all the observers at once, not as they are seen by one of them but as
they are for themselves and in the absolute of their lives,
these solitary durations, no longer able to be applied to
each other, measured by each other, would offer no further
displacement and thus would cease to fragmentize the universe of time. Now this restoration of all the durations together, which is not possible at their interior source, since
each of us coincides only with his own, occurs, Bergson
said, when the embodied subjects interperceive one another,
when their perceptive fields intersect and envelop each
other, when they see each other in the act of perceiving
the same world. Perception poses in its own order a uni-

versal duration, and the formulas which permit passage from one system of reference to another are, like all physics, secondary objectifications which cannot determine what is meaningful in our experience either of embodied subjects or of the totality of being. This was the outline of a philosophy which bases the universal on the mystery of perception and proposes, as Bergson has justly said, not to fly above perception but to penetrate it.

Perception to Bergson is the totality of these "complementary powers of understanding" which alone are the measure of being and which, opening us to it, "see themselves at work in the operations of nature." If only we know how to perceive life, the being of life will show itself to be of the same type as these simple and indivisible beings for which the things under our eyes, older than any manufactured thing, offer us the model, and the operation of life will appear to us as a sort of perception. When we note that life, after long preparations, assembles a visual apparatus on a line of evolution and, sometimes, the same apparatus on divergent lines of evolution, we think we see a single movement, like that of my own hand, behind the convergent details; and the "march toward vision" in the species hangs on the total act of perception as *Matter and Memory* has described it. There Bergson refers to it expressly. It is this, he says, which descends more or less into organisms. That does not mean that the world of life is a human representation, nor, moreover, that human perception is a cosmic product: it means that the original perception that we find in ourselves and the one which shows

through in evolution as its interior principle are inter-
twined, and overlap or are bound each to the other.
Whether we find in ourselves the entry to the world or lay
hold on the interior life, always there is the same tension
between one duration and another duration which borders
it from without.

We see well enough in the Bergson of 1907, the intuition
of intuitions, the central intuition, and it is far from being,
as has mistakenly been said, a "je ne sais quoi," an act
of uncontrollable genius. The source to which he goes and
from which his philosophy takes its meaning—why would
it not be simply the architectonics of his interior landscape,
the manner in which his gaze encounters things or life, his
bond with himself, nature, and living beings, his contact
with being in us and outside of us? And for this inexhaustible intuition, was not the best "mediating image" the
visible and existing world itself, as *Matter and Memory* described it? Even when he passed upwards toward the transcendent, Bergson did not think himself able to attain it
except by a sort of "perception." Life, at any rate, which,
below us, always solves problems in a way different than
we do, resembles the human spirit less than it does this
imminent or eminent vision that Bergson glimpsed in
things. Perceived being is that spontaneous or natural being that the Cartesians did not see because they sought
being against a background of non-being, and, Bergson
says, because they lacked the being necessary to "conquer
nonexistence." He describes a preconstituted being, always
felt to be on the edge of our reflections, always already

there to disarm the agony and lostness that are on the verge of birth.

It is indeed hard to know why he never thought of history from within, as he thought of life from within, why he never set himself there, too, to the study of the simple and indivisible acts which, for each period and each event, establish the order of partial facts. In positing that each period is all it can be, an entire event, all one action, and that preromanticism, for example, is a postromantic illusion, Bergson seems to refuse once and for all the notion of historical depth. Péguy, however, tried to describe the emergence of the event—when some begin and others respond—and also historical completion, the response of one generation to what was begun by another. He saw the essence of history in this meeting of individuals and time, which is difficult, since the deed, the work, the past are inaccessible in their simplicity to those who see them from outside, since years are needed to create the history of this revolution which was made in a day; an infinite commentary does not exhaust this page which was written in an hour. The chances of error, of deviation, of failure, are great. But it is the cruel law for those who write, who act, or who live in public—that is to say, finally, of all embodied spirits—to expect, from others or from successors, another carrying out of what they are doing; another and the same, says Péguy profoundly, because these also are men, because in this substitution, they have made themselves similar to the originator. There is in this, he says, a sort of scandal, but "a justified scandal" and consequently something "mysterious." Meaning refashions itself at the risk of destroying itself; it is a fluid meaning, well conformed to the Bergsonian definition of meaning, which is "less a thing thought than the movement of thought, less a movement than a direction." In this network of challenges and responses, where the beginning metamorphoses and completes itself, there is a duration which belongs to no one and to everyone, a "public duration," the "rhythm and real speed of the world event," which would be, said Péguy, the subjects of a true sociology. He had shown, by this, that a Bergsonian intuition of history is possible.

But Bergson, who said of Péguy in 1915 that he knew his "essential thought," nevertheless did not follow him on this point. For Bergson, precious little credit can be given to the notion of the "historical record" nor of challenging generations and responding generations: there is only the heroic call of individual to individual, a mystique without a "mystical body." For him, there is no single fabric where good and evil dwell together; there are natural societies breached by irruptions of the mystical. During the long years when he was preparing the *Two Sources* he seems not to have been saturated in history as he was saturated in life; he did not find at work in history, as once in life, "complementary powers of understanding" in close touch with our own duration. He remains too optimistic in regard to that which concerns the individual and his ability to rediscover the source of things, too pessimistic in regard to what touches the social life, to admit, as in the above definition of history, a "justified scandal."

And perhaps this holding on to opposites is reflective of the whole doctrine; the fact is that *La Pensée et le Mouvant*, at much the same period as the *Two Sources*, rectifies in the sense of a clean delimitation—not without "overlappings," it is true—the relationships of implication that the *Introduction to Metaphysics* had established between philosophy and science, intuition and intelligence, spirit and matter. If decidedly there is for Bergson no mystery of history, if he does not, like Péguy, see men involved with each other, if he is not aware of the prevenient presence of symbols around us and of the profound changes of which they are the vehicles—if, for example, he finds, in the origins of democracy, only its "evangelical essence" and the Christianity of Kant and Rousseau—this way he has of cutting short certain possibilities and arresting the final implications of his work must express a basic preference; it is part of his philosophy and we ought to try to understand it.

That in him which is opposed to any philosophy of mediation and of history is one of the earliest elements of his thought, the certainty of a "half-divine" state in which man knows neither lostness nor anguish. Meditation on history modified this conviction without lessening it. At the time of *Creative Evolution* the philosophical intuition of the natural being sufficed to get rid of the false problems of non-being. In the *Two Sources* "divine man" has become "inaccessible," but it is always he against whom Bergson puts human history in perspective. The natural contact with being, joy, peace—quietism—remain essential with Bergson; they are only transferred from the *de jure* generaliz-able experience of the philosopher to the exceptional ex-perience of the mystic, which opens on another nature, and on a second positivity, which are boundless. It is the di-vision of nature into unreconciled *natura naturans* and *natura naturata* which in the *Two Sources,* brings about the distinction between God and his action on the world, left implicit in the previous works. Bergson certainly does not say *Deus sive Natura,* but if he does not say it it is be-cause God is another nature. At the moment when he fi-nally separates the "transcendent cause" from its "earthly delegation" it is again the word of nature which comes under his pen. In God is concentrated all that was truly active and creative in this world, which finally, is only "arrest" or "created thing." But the relationship of man with this Super-Nature remains the direct relationship that the previous books found between intuition and natural being. There is the simple act which made the human spe-cies; there is the simple and simplifying act of God in the mystique; there is no simple act which founds the domain of history and of evil. That truly is only an interspace. It is better to say that man is made of two simple principles, than to say he is double. History, oscillating between *natura naturata* and *natura naturans,* has no true substance. Cer-tainly it is not accursed, the universe remains a "machine for making gods," and that is not after all impossible, since *natura naturata* has its source in *natura naturans.* But if one day the machine to make gods succeeds in what it has always failed to do it will be as though arrested creation

sence. The metaphysical attributes which seem to determine him are, Bergson says, like all determinants, nega-
tions. Even if against all possibility they became visible,
no religious man would recognize in them the God to
whom he prays. The God of Bergson is a being as unique
as the universe, an immense *this,* and Bergson has extended
even into theology his promise of a philosophy made for
actual being, and which applies only to it. If one in imag-
inative terms compares the actual with the ideal, it must
be admitted, he says, that "the whole of things could have
been much superior to what it is." No one can have it that
the death of someone is an element in the making of
the best of all possible worlds. But it is not only the solutions of classical theodicy that are false, it is its problems
which have no meaning in the order where Bergson places
himself, which is that of the radical contingency. There is
no question here of the conceived world or of a conceived
God, but of the existing world and of existing God; and
that in us which knows this order is more or less beneath
our opinions and our statements. No one can keep men
from loving their life, miserable as it might be. This vital
judgment retrieves life and God from accusations as well
as from justifications. And if one insists on understanding how *natura naturans* has been able to produce *natura
naturata* in which it has not truly realized itself; why, at
least provisionally, the creative force has arrested itself;
what obstacle it has met and how an obstacle can be insur-
mountable for it; Bergson would admit—with reservations
as to other planets where perhaps life has succeeded better

—that his philosophy does not answer such questions, but it does not have to ask them, being ultimately not a cosmogony—not even (as it almost became) the integration and differentiation of one system—but the deliberately partial, discontinuous, almost empirical groping for many centers of being.

On the whole, Péguy is right when he says that this philosophy has "for the first time . . . attracted attention to what being itself had in its own right and to the articulation of the present." Nascent being, from which no representation separates me, which contains in advance the views, however conflicting, however incompatible, that we can take of it, which stands before us, younger and older than the possible and the necessary, and which, once born, can never cease to exist and will continue to exist in the depths of other presents: we know that at the beginning of the century the books which rediscovered this forgotten being and its powers were experienced as a renaissance, a liberation of philosophy, and their value in this respect is intact. It would have been fine if the same view of origins had then been focused on passions, events, techniques, law, language, literature, to find their own spiritual nature, taking them as monuments and prophecies of hieratic man, as cryptograms of a questioning spirit. Bergson believed in verification and in invention; he did not believe in interrogative thought. But, even in this restriction of his scope, he is exemplary in his fidelity to what he has seen. In the religious conversations of the last years, when his philosophy found itself, in terms of experimental contribution and benevolent aid, included, by some, in the Thomist framework—as if it were not clear that something essential is lost when one adds to it—what strikes me is the tranquility with which Bergson, in the very moment when he gives to Catholicism a personal assent and a moral adherence, maintains his method in philosophy. After having held strictly to his direction through the storms, he held to it during the final reconciliations. His efforts and his works, which restored philosophy to the present and showed what can today be an approach to being, also teach us how a man of an earlier moment remained indomitable. They showed that one must not claim anything which cannot be "shown," that one must know how to wait and to keep others waiting, to displease and even to please, to be oneself, to be true— and that, moreover, among men, this firmness is not in the least despised, since, in seeking the truth, it moreover, gave birth to Bergsonism.

by Jean Wahl

(AT THE SORBONNE)

In a kind of silence I see the visage of Henri Bergson arise from the past; a zone of silence surrounded him, whether one visited him or went to the Collège de France to hear him speak of Spencer, Berkeley, Plotinus, or Spinoza, to whom he was perhaps closer than at first appeared. I have had this joy, this privilege, of contact with a great philosopher. Today I would not want to separate him from those who were his friends; I should like to mention William James, the great American philosopher; Le Roy; I should like also to mention—but they have already been referred to—Péguy, Thibaudet, and Whitehead, and I especially recall a conversation when two names were spoken by Whitehead during my visit, that of Bergson and that of Gilson, whom he cherished also.

I belong or have belonged to many groups which may be considered hostile to Bergson, and I have liked them all very much: first the École Normale; it was not very good, in 1907 or 1908 (I hesitate to recall that far-off year), to write an article in favor of Bergson. To class one-

self among the Bergsonians was very bad. Today we are
happy, at the Sorbonne, to celebrate Bergson's memory, in
this magnificent amphitheater. The Sorbonne was not always friendly to Bergson, and Bergson remembered it. Recently a journal echoed these memories. In literary groups,
the *Nouvelle Revue Française,* on the whole, certainly not
the first generation but the second, was hostile to Bergson,
aside from Thibaudet who admired him greatly and wrote
a very fine book on him, which stands beside that of Jankélévitch. And I am allied with the philosophers of existence. Two of the most illustrious philosophers of existence are among us, and perhaps the public has noticed all
their reservations on the philosophy of Bergson, which at
the same time they admire.

I remember some conversations with Bergson on science,
on philosophy; I admired the multiplicity of approaches
in his thought. It would be necessary, if we were to study
him—we hardly possess sufficient time to do so—it would
be necessary to distinguish his critical methods, his cri-
tiques of ideas, his dissociations of ideas, and also his
hypotheses, and, too, his way of following facts and lines
of facts, of establishing provisional certainties, of making
pseudo-problems disappear by pointing out common postu-
lates in doctrines apparently opposed, of also establishing,
afterward, definite certainties. It would be necessary to
study a whole vocabulary: *le mouvant, le vécu, le se fai-
sant.* His first book, *Les Données immédiates,* is an effort
toward immediate facts, because dialectically, if one may
use this term for him, he thinks that the immediate should

be conquered. But this conquered immediate is the absolute, and, in opposition to the agonosticism of most of his contemporaries, Bergson wanted to show that we are, in many ways, in touch with the absolute. We are in touch with it even in science, which places us before an absolute that is matter, in the perception that places us in the object itself, at point 0, as he says, of the object. And, beyond this, there are absolutes of the spirit. So that, if the word were not used for other forms of doctrine, one would willingly say that there was a gnosticism in Bergson, an affirmation of the knowability of the absolute. He always wanted to find the pure and the full: the pure, by his methods of carrying through to the limit; and the full, for he thinks that concepts will never fill this plenitude of intuition; and so he presents to us a multiple world, with images such as he painted at the beginning of *Matter and Memory*, thus going beyond realism and idealism. It was something unheard of at that moment in philosophy, an effort to go beyond the two opposed doctrines. Above, there are all the projects, tensions of the intellect, and below, there is the *élan*, the *élan vital*. Many difficulties arise from the confrontation between the theory of *Time and Free Will* and the theory of pure memory in *Matter and Memory*, where a new dimension, in depth, of the past appears. Words like "action" and "life" successively take on different aspects, often opposed. In the social dimension, disparaged to begin with, we see born later, with the support of productive intuition, sublime forms. And I remember Bergson's article on "Philosophical Intuition," which is for every historian of philosophy a lesson, that he should not stop with the structures of systems, or contradictions, or the use of words in multiple meanings, so that he will be enabled to see the unity of vision; and I believe one might say—I have already used the word "dialectic"—I believe one might say that Bergson had a destructive dialectic, a descending dialectic, an ascending dialectic, and finally a destruction of dialectic by the vision of the single movement which is at the depths of the whole universe.

Few thinkers have been so daring as Bergson, for he gave us a description of the whole universe, as he viewed it, each time taking his departure from certain precise facts, which he attempted—following the scientists, but criticizing scientists when necessary—to establish as precisely as possible. I have once thought that if one had to name the four great philosophers one could say: Socrates, Plato—taking them together,—Descartes, Kant, and Bergson; that is to say, the philosophers who turned us toward ourselves, who, each in his own way, said, "Know thyself." But at the same time we have seen that he places us in the absolute; we are not separated from the world, from the universe. Perhaps he goes beyond the ontologies which have succeeded him, founded on the pseudo-ideas of non-being and being, and he takes his place among the very great philosophers. He reunites two of the first philosophers: Heraclitus and Parmenides, Heraclitus by motion and the affirmation of motion, Parmenides by the affirmation of the fullness of being. No disquietude in Bergson? But there is always the danger of a set-back or a total engulfment of the *élan vital:* there is the danger of the endless succession of dual frenzies.

Confidence in the human *élan?* Yes, without doubt; but Bergson always preserves in himself, mastered, a profound disquietude about this life—even a certain misanthropy. And at the same time he sees that, beyond, he can have something; he questions himself in spite of all; on his table I always saw Madame Guyon's *Les Torrents,* for it is through Madame Guyon that he was led to the understanding he acquired of mystical experience.

It seems to me that meditation on Bergson can serve us as a purification. It can exorcise. "Bergson et Nous," that is the theme of this gathering, but I would prefer to stress the accent on Bergson; we should question him, question ourselves before him; and in questioning myself on him and before him I see in evidence two of the kinds of profound memory that he distinguished: the memory of Bergson before me, in the past, and then what he is in my own duration. There is Bergson as he was, and he is present as he was, he is here at this moment. And thus, he is a part of the durations of us all, we philosophers who are here, and it is simply this that I wished to say this evening.

thereafter. I hope therefore that it is a question of a re-
newal of Bergsonian thought, and that we shall not wait
another century to speak of it again. The second way of
not being Bergsonian is to treat Bergson like a historical
specimen, to resay what he has said instead of doing as he
has done; or to "place" Bergsonism, instead of rethinking
Bergson as Bergson wanted to be rethought. These two
pseudo-Bergsonisms, that of the anniversary-Bergsonians
and that of historians, suggest to us the two principal points
of this short speech.

And first of all, the necessity of thinking of Bergson in
the Bergsonian manner, as we believe that he wished us to
do. Bergsonism is a maximalist philosophy, which demands the total adherence of the heart and of the spirit.
For Bergson there are only utter totalities, organic totalities; no vacuum comes to deplete the positive fullness in
which we live; all that exists is complete, viable, all-suffi-
cient to itself. It is necessary, however, that these totalities
be equal in dignity; their moral weight, their value, their
quality, their density, their profundity differ; these in-
equalities give the totalization its reason for existence and
its scope. The totalization is possible although each being
at each instant may be total! Freedom is this totalization
itself. The free act is the act into which, according to Bergson, man puts his whole self: it is the decision in which the
wholeness of his person figures; on it the personal past
presses, with all its weight and all its richness. It must,
then, be understood that freedom moves in the same direction as life, which tends continually to fill out, con-

Ethics, define the σπουδαῖος, the serious man, as the one who desires with his whole soul, κατὰ πᾶσαν τὴν ψυχήν? This expression is not only Aristotelian and Platonic: the Old and New Testaments also use it. It is in Deuteronomy, for the first time, and then in the Book of Isaiah, that God demands that he be loved with the whole soul; and later the apostles, varying the formula, say that it is necessary to love God "with all one's strength," ἐξ ὁλης τῆς ἰσχύος, "with all one's understanding," ἐξ ὁλης τῆς συνέσεως, "with all one's mind," ἐν ὁλη τῇ διανοία. In short, God is the one to whom man is related not with the slightest bit of his soul, but with all his power, all his knowledge, and all his will, therefore in a full manner. Truth is not only an object of contemplation but an object of fulfillment and a true sustenance: thus the Bergsonian intuition is not only knowledge but ecstatic identification with the object: truth, for Bergson, as for the Scriptures, wishes to be known and loved with an undivided heart, that is to say, by a heart pure, simple, transparent, and whole as a crystal.

In fact, Bergsonism is not a philosophy like the others, for it demands of us, if not a genuine initiation, at least particular ways of approach. We know that Bergson spoke of a twisting of the will on itself: this twisting implies a violent and radical reform of our habits, an inversion of conceptual method, and, in all, a true interior renovation. There was needed, then, for the approach, a new heart, and not a little piece of this heart, not merely an auricle or a ventricle, but the whole heart. It had to be truly a pure heart. It is the philosophical act itself which demands this oneself" is much conjugated today, and usually in a minor and notional and oblique sense: for, to the knights of verbal engagement, to engage oneself means to engage oneself to engage oneself; it is an engagement with a view of engagement, an engagement to the secondary or tertiary power. Bergsonism rediscovers the innocent efficacy of the Act. A phrase is often repeated in *The Two Sources of Morality and Religion,* a phrase to which we do not pay enough attention: "Do not listen to what they say, look at what they do." This warning shows first the value that Bergson attaches to experience in general, to all that is perceived or perceivable; but there is something else: there is the idea that the language of acts—and this language of acts may be the word itself, when, for example, it is a question of courageously saying, "No"—is an especially eloquent and convincing manner of expressing oneself. In the *Nichomachean Ethics* Aristotle, speaking of Eudoxus of Cnidus, says that it is better to be an austere hedonist than a depraved rigorist—because what counts is acts and not words; because it is the "to do" or "not to do" which matters. To act as one speaks, or even to act without speaking, such would be the motto of Bergsonian wisdom. In that, too, Bergson stretches out his hand to Tolstoi, for whom the return to the immediate, the return to things themselves, was the first imperative of a vital Christianity. Did not Tolstoi wish to put this astringent wisdom into application at Yasnaya Polyana? Besides, ethics, for him, is mingled with hagiography, which recounts the *res gestae* of the saints. The saint, according to *The Two Sources of*

Morality and Religion, performs an action by his very
presence itself and not by his sermons; for the important
thing is not to "say" but to "do." Here is what Bergsonism
helps us to understand better: there are things—and they
are the most important of all and the most precious in life
—which are not made to be spoken of but which are made
to be done. One might say that this is so of all philosophy.
Not to speak of philosophy at all, no, but to act it, that is
incumbent on us; but philosophers, avoiding the problems
themselves in favor of "lectern" philosophy, prefer to
speak of each other and never to go beyond the prelimi-
naries. Bergson makes us aware for the first time of the
idea that philosophy is an act that everyone performs on
his own account, as if he were alone in the world, as if he
were the first to perform it, as if no one had ever performed
it before him. Naturally, this is not true, but it is necessary
to act as if it were; in that, the philosophical act resembles
love; he who loves does again what millions of men have
done before him; and nevertheless he experiences what he
does as a wholly new thing, unheard of, original, and ver-
nal; for him, to do again is to do; for him, to begin again
is to begin; he who loves for the first time is in his own
way an inventor and an inspired improviser. Did not Descartes himself urge us to that re-creation which is creation?
The intention of Bergson was not that we do again *what*
he did, but that we do again as he did; it is Bergsonian to
look in the direction Bergson points out to us, but it is not
at all so to carp at Bergsonism, at the place it occupies, at
the pigeonhole in which it is convenient to place it. It is in

and sudden surprise which is already inherent in stringent seeking. Bergson, in *Creative Evolution*, expresses it somewhat this way: the intelligence is capable of searching for something but by itself can find nothing; and, vice versa, instinct finds it immediately and unerringly, but can find one thing only: that for which it is made. Well, only intuition is capable of both, a simultaneous finding and seeking. Better than that, by the very act of seeking, it has already found. "You would not seek me if you had not found me." It is, thus, the heuristic intention which is itself the finding; the thing sought was already found, but it was necessary to think of it. And thus man begins with the discovery, that is to say, at the end! To begin, it is necessary to begin, and we do not learn how to begin. To begin requires only courage. Indeed, we would say, modifying the "Velle non discitur" of Seneca: *Incipire non discitur*—because there are no recipes for creating, for beginning, and for giving, but only for imitating, continuing, and conserving. In that, Bergson rejoins Lequier, according to whom freedom is a beginning for itself. Two solutions may permit us to exorcise the Eleatic Gorgon which paralyzes our consciousness, to find again with a whole soul and by immediate decision the whole simple truth. One is called love: the thread of Ariadne which guided the lost Theseus through the labyrinth, that is love; it is amorous inspiration which leads Theseus forth from the maze; it is the beloved woman, the second person *par excellence*, who unravels the tortuous problem. The other solution is an even simpler discovery: it consists in flying above what one cannot resolve, in treating problems as though they did not exist; it was thus, as we noted with the pseudo-paralytic; it is thus with Dedalus, himself confined in the labyrinth he has made, entangled in his artificial aporia, incapable of unraveling the imbroglio he has so carefully tangled. And suddenly the idea comes to him of flying through the air, in the face of the astounded monsters: he circumvents the problem by making wings for himself; he resolves it by abolishing it through levitation and acts as if the labyrinth did not exist. And not only does this decision mobilize and restore the consciousness which has been spellbound by the sorceries of accursed philosophers (so Eugénio d'Ors calls Zeno of Elea), but the freed man also frees the slaves around him. The saint and the hero of *The Two Sources of Morality and Religion* are in a way an exhortation to movement, a conversion of man to the right kind of movement. They remind man that the right kind of movement is, in effect, an entirely simple thing. Freedom acts somewhat in the manner of that magnetic stone of which Plato speaks in *Ion;* freedom is not only freedom to possess an isolated freedom in itself; freedom delivers others; freedom is liberating. Free men, like generous men, set men free not at all by what they say—like lecturers—nor by what they write—like literary men—but by what they do, like heroes, and, even more, like saints, by what they are. Heroes do not lecture on heroism any more than nightingales lecture on arpeggios, but nightingales perform arpeggios and demonstrate the existence of the arpeggio by performing it; the hero sets up the possibility of the impossible by doing the impossible; the impossibility becomes as simple as hello and goodby; it is the person, in himself and whole,

Bibliography

WORKS OF BERGSON

—— *Quid de loco Aristoteles sensuerit.* Paris, Alcan, 1889.

—— *Essai sur les Données immédiates de la Conscience.* Paris, Alcan, 1889.

—— *Matière et Mémoire.* Paris, Alcan, 1896.

—— *Le Rire: Essai sur la signification du comique.* Paris, Alcan, 1900.

—— *Note sur l'origine psychologique de notre croyance à la loi de causalité.* Congrès de Philosophie, 1900.

—— *L'Evolution Créatrice.* Paris, Alcan, 1907.

—— *L'Energie Spirituelle.* Paris, Alcan, 1909.

—— "La Philosophie," *La Science Française.* Paris, Larousse, 1915.

—— *Durée et Simultanéité: A propos de la Théorie d'Einstein.* Paris, Alcan, 1922.

—— *Les deux Sources de la Morale et de la Religion.* Paris, Alcan, 1932.

—— *La Pensée et le Mouvant.* Paris, Alcan, 1934.

(A recent, only partially complete collection of Bergson's works was published in 1946 by Editions Albert Skira of Geneva under the general title, *Oeuvres Complètes d'Henri Bergson.*)

RECENT FULL-LENGTH WORKS ON BERGSON
IN FRENCH AND IN ENGLISH

Adès, Albert. *Adès chez Bergson: Reliques inconnues d'une amitié.* Paris, N. Fortin et ses fils, 1949.

Adolphe, Lydie. *La Dialectique des Images chez Bergson*. Paris, Presses Universitaires de la France, 1951.

—— *La Philosophie Religieuse de Bergson*. Paris, Presses Universitaires de France, 1946.

—— *L'Univers Bergsonien*. Paris, Edit. du Vieux Colombier, 1955.

Alexander, Ian W. *Bergson: Philosopher of Reflection*. New York, Hillary House, 1957.

Arbour, Roméo. *Henri Bergson et les Lettres français*. Paris, Libr. José Corti, 1955.   *N*

Bayer, Raymond. *L'Esthétique de Bergson*. Paris, Presses Universitaires de France, 1943.

Benrubi, Isaak. *Souvenirs sur Henri Bergson*. Paris, Delachaux et Niestlé, 1942.

Bergson et le Bergsonisme, ed. Paris, Beauchesne, 1947.

Bonhomme, Bary B. *Educational Implications of the Philosophy of Henri Bergson*. Washington, D.C.: The Catholic University Press, 1944.

Bréhier, Émile. *Notice sur la Vie et les Travaux de Henri Bergson* Paris, Impr. de Firmin-Didot, 1946.

Challaye, Félicien. *Bergson*. Paris, Mellottée, 1947.

Chevalier, Jacques. *Bergson*. Paris, Plon, 1941.

—— *Bergson et le Père Pouget*. Paris, Plon, 1954.

Controverses Bergsoniennes, ed. Paris, Armand Colin, 1941.

Cresson, André. *Bergson: sa vie, son oeuvre*. Paris, Presses Universitaires, 1941.

Delattre, Floris. *Ruskin et Bergson*. Oxford, The Clarendon Press, 1947.

Delhomme, Jeanne. *Vie et Conscience de la Vie: Essai sur Bergson*. Paris, Presses Universitaires de France, 1954.

Etudes Bergsoniennes: Hommage à Henri Bergson, edit. Paris, Presses Universitaires, 1942.

Fleury, René Albert. *Bergson et la Quantité*. Paris, Copy-Odéon, 1941.

Gillouin, René, ed. *Henri Bergson: Choix de textes*. Paris, Soc. des Edit. Louis Michaud, 194?.

Heidsieck, François. *Henri Bergson et la notion d'espace*. Paris, Le Cercle du Livre, 1957.

Henri Bergson. *Neuchatel: La Baconnière*. 1941.

Hertrich, Charles. *Le Génie de Bergson*. St.-Etienne, Edit. des Flambeaux, 1940.

—— *Qu'est-ce que la vie? d'après Bergson*. St.-Etienne, Edit. de Flambeaux, 1942.

Husson, León. *L'Intellectualisme de Bergson*. Paris, Presses Universitaires de France, 1947.

Le Roy, E., ed. *Bergson et le Bergsonisme*. Paris, Archives de la Philosophie, 1947.

Les Études Bergsoniennes, vol. I, edit. Paris, Albin Michel, 1948.

Les Études Bergsoniennes, vol. II, edit. Paris, Albin Michel, 1949.

Les Études Bergsoniennes, vol. III, edit. Paris, Albin Michel, 1952.

Les Études Bergsoniennes, vol. IV., edit. Paris, Albin Michel, 1956.

Mariettie, Angèle. *Les Formes du Mouvement chez Bergson*. Le Puy, Impr. Moderne, 1953.

Maritain, Jacques. *De Bergson à Thomas d'Aquin*. Paris, Hartmann, 1947.

Meyer, François. *La Pensée de Bergson*. Grenoble, Bordas Frères, 1944.

—— *Pour connaître la pensée de Bergson*. Paris, Bordas, 1948.

Mossé-Bastide, Rose-Marie, edit. Henri Bergson: *Ecrits et paroles*. Paris, Presses Universitaires de France, 1957.

—— *Bergson éducateur*. Paris, Presses Universitaires de France, 1955.

Mullen, Mary D. *Essence and Operation in the Teaching of St.*

Thomas in Some Modern Philosophies. Washington, D.C., The Catholic University of America Press, 1941.

Politzer, Georges. *Le Bergsonisme, une mystification philosophique.* Paris, Edit. Sociales, 1947.

Scharfstein, Ben-Ami. *Roots of Bergson's Philosophy.* New York, Columbia University Press, 1943.

Sundén, Hjalmar. *La Théorie Bergsonienne de la Religion.* Upsala, Almqvist and Wiksells, 1940.

Valéry, Paul. *Henri Bergson.* Paris, Domat-Montchrestien, 1945.

Verdène, Georges. *Bergson le Révolté ou l'Ascension d'une âme.* Genève, P.-F. Perret-Gentil, 1942.

The editor is grateful to the following for giving their kind permission to quote the passages in Dr. Starkie's contribution: Holt, Rinehart and Winston, Inc., New York, for the quotations from Henri Bergson, *The Two Sources of Morality and Religion;* Random House, New York, for the quotation from Marcel Proust, *The Past Recaptured.* The quotations from *Laughter* are from the book *Comedy,* copyright © 1956 by Wylie Sypher, which contains *Laughter* by Henri Bergson, reprinted by permission of Doubleday and Company.